Finding a Language
Autonomy and learning in school

Peter Medway

WITHDRAWN

Finding a Language
Autonomy and learning in school
Peter Medway

Finding a Language
Autonomy and learning in school
Peter Medway

Writers and Readers in association with **Chameleon**

Published 1980 by Writers and Readers Publishing Cooperative,
25 Nassington Road, London NW3 in association with
Chameleon, 22 Bicester Road, Richmond, Surrey.

Printed and bound in Great Britain by Whitstable Litho Ltd.,
Whitstable, Kent.

case ISBN 0 906495 40 7
paper ISBN 0 906459 41 5

Contents

Introduction

'We moved on to this place next to this banking. We saw little ditches where the rabbits had been digging to get roots. This is what they ate when they didn't feel like eating grass. Then we would see starts of holes, then we saw one big hole. Toby dived towards the hole. This was another good sign — this meant we were going to have a good time. Toby started to dig. He was really going. We could tell there was a rabbit in the hole because there was all shit round the hole. Toby dug for ages. Then he came out and Jan went in to dig. It was like a shift at the pit — they kept digging and changing over. Then Eddy said, "Come out, dogs. Let's have a look at what's going on."

We had a look at the hole where they had been but the dogs had covered the hole up, so we decided to move on up the banking. We spread along in a line and when I was walking I came to this hill, so I started to climb up this hill. Just as I got to the top a rabbit shot over the hill behind me. I shouted to Eddy. Eddy started to run after it but it just pulled away and went into the brambles. Toby dived in and Jan covered the entrance from where the rabbit had run. We all spread out round the brambles. Toby started to bark. This was a sign that he was on the trail of it. Like a flash of lightning the rabbit shot from the brambles but Eddy stuck his boot out and the rabbit run into it and knocked itself out. So to kill it off Eddy gave it one big blow to the back of the neck and the rabbit was dead.

By this time it was getting towards eight o'clock, so we set off home. By now the nights were getting dark early and the morning was not getting light till about 7.30. So we decided to stop going until next year.'

I had started out as an English teacher, but my two previous jobs had been in an integrated studies department and on a Schools Council project concerned with language in all subjects. Now I was in school again, this time as head of English. It was good to be back in both respects: back in the classroom of course, but more especially working again with straight English. Kids turning their experience into art — what more interesting process could one be associated with? Poetry, fiction, children reflecting on their lives, a rich local culture for them to express — there was a lot to be said for it. And there were aspects of the other subjects which I was glad to be free of.

It wasn't long, though, before I found myself involved again with the wider curriculum, as 'co-ordinator' of humanities. And already I was pleased to be getting outside English. I realised that in that year or so I had missed dealing with inquiry and understanding, with satisfying curiosities about how the world works and with seeking out causes and patterns in human society. English had turned out to be less than completely satisfying; it didn't seem to add up to a viable educational enterprise on its own. Teaching English felt like fighting with one hand tied behind my back.

There was more to be got out of a mining community's love of dogs and hunting than a vigorous celebration of it in a piece of writing, worthwhile though that was; and there was more to be got out of history and sociology than abstract schemes and handed-down facts. It seemed that English and the other humanities disciplines each needed to be conducted in the light of the other; and both had to be influenced in special ways by the particular strengths and needs of students from a strongly rooted, largely working-class community. This book arises out of our attempts to get right that three-fold relationship: English, humanities, working-class students. In terms of chronology, we moved in the senior part of the school (14—16) from a separate subject timetable to a combined humanities scheme; integrated studies already existed lower down. But this is not a history: the book's purpose is to share the sort of arguments and considerations which we found ourselves confronting, and then the outcomes of some innovations that we introduced because of them. Part 1 therefore presents a general line of thinking, one not specifically related to the circumstances of our own school though supported with examples drawn from there, while Part 2 is a report on the integrated course we introduced.

I would like to thank the students who have allowed me to quote their work and those who helped me by recording their comments on tape. In written pieces it seemed best on balance to regularise the spelling and to supply punctuation where its lack was likely to cause problems to the reader. I have given fictitious names to the school, the teachers and most of the students.

1 English and the curriculum

I have never seen an account of English teaching which justifies it in the same terms that can apply to the other academic subjects. English on the one hand and history, science etc. on the other are explained by different educational philosophies that are not so much in conflict as unrelated. English teachers tend to write for each other, and outsiders can only understand what they are saying by leaving behind their own language and frame of reference and taking on those of the English teachers. This seems unsatisfactory, since schools ought to have educational aims which inform the whole institution and to which the different subjects contribute. The problem becomes a practical one when there are schemes to 'integrate' English with other (usually humanities) subjects. Is it an inescapable problem, or can we see a way of accounting for the different subjects that makes it possible to think of them all as part of the same educational game?

As an example of the problem, two key terms in the language of teachers of the other subjects, 'knowledge' and 'learning', are rarely used about English. English teachers do not describe what happens in their lessons as 'learning' or what their pupils end up with as 'knowledge'; or, if they do, it is only when referring to subsidiary aspects of the work such as spelling or literary facts, and not to what they regard as the central activities. 'Knowledge' and 'learning' are tied in people's minds to facts and information, and the reason why English teachers avoid the terms is that they do not see themselves as dealing with facts. Indeed, it is sometimes said that English is 'a subject without a content'. As long as the prevalent terminology and explanations serve mainly to draw attention in this way to the *differences* between English and the rest, it will be difficult to relate them to each other in a rational way.

A promising place to start the search for a common basis might be the 'content' of English. Now to say that English has no content is plainly absurd. Students in English lessons are constantly talking, writing and reading, and not — in good English lessons at any rate — in a ritualised or mechanical way but with all the appearance of making and receiving real communications; all this communication must be about something, and that something, we could say, is the content of English.

So we cannot say that there is no content. We might, however, say that this content has no obvious coherence, in the way that the content of geography has; and English teachers will indeed sometimes say that it is conceivable for their lessons to be about almost anything. But a content is none the less a content for being hard to define, and in fact the predominance of the content is one of the features of present-day English practice which non-initiates find most disturbing and puzzling. There was a time when English was quite clearly about nouns and verbs and words — about English, in fact: now the concern in English lessons seems to be, by reading, talking, writing and so on, to contemplate thoroughly or to get to understand some *phenomenon*, such as old people, the circumstances in which one experiences fear or the way pigeons behave. The content seems to have taken over. Moreover, although it may lack conceptual unity, this content appears to be relatively settled and established: anyone looking at English teaching and its published materials, broadcasts etc., would quickly be able to tell you what English is about, namely: the family, animals, relationships between children and adults, authority, crime and punishment, war . . . The list is not a closed one, but in the majority of its elements is constant enough to merit being called the content of English.

English teachers have their explanation, and it is a good one. They claim that the shift of attention from the English language to aspects of the real world is more apparent than real. The concern with language is still paramount, only it is now realised in ways that are more effective than direct instruction in the features of English. Children (and adults for that matter) become skilful in their use of language by using it in demanding situations to achieve purposes that they are committed to and in which success will bring satisfactions, whether the purposes are personal or public, serious or light-hearted. One such motivating purpose can be the desire to understand something and feel you have got to the bottom of it and grasped the significance of all its aspects — whether the something is a moral problem, an incident observed, a physical phenomenon, a state of mind, an interesting person or an idea. It is this sort of purpose that the English teacher predominantly seeks to mobilise so that language will be brought into play in fulfilling it and thereby be exercised and extended. Clearly, the pupils must feel that the consideration being given to a topic is serious, as the necessary struggle to express understandings in words will not be motivated when the situation is seen as a mere language exercise, and that is why so many English lessons appear to be singlemindedly about something other than English — about content, in fact. The sought-after extension of competence in English can only come from genuine attempts to engage with aspects of reality.

In other words, from the attempt to *learn*: there is no reason to deny this label to the substantial and worthwhile changes in consciousness that results from language activities in English. The fact that the learning, unlike that which occurs in, say, geography, does not primarily derive from inputs of new information, clearly does not stop it being learning (though it may prevent teachers and students from recognising it as such — as may their preoccupation with the language progress that accompanies it). And in this light, English begins to look more like the other subjects: in the lessons of all of them there is a content — some aspect of reality — that is taken seriously; in all of them learning, in the sense of a fuller grasp of reality, takes place. Thus the whole academic curriculum, and not only that part of it which is outside English, is in some sense about knowledge. Nor is this such a novel idea: traditionally, reading literature and being a writer were thought to lead, not to language development, but to wisdom; writers and poets were men and women who not only knew how to use words but understood about life.

In fact, English can no longer even maintain that it is special in its concern for language development. Those ways of using language which have been found, in English, to bring about linguistic competence are also the ways to get to understand things, and there is no reason why those ways should be exclusively associated with the particular content which English has earmarked as its own; it makes sense, in fact, for other subjects equally to encourage language, in the interests of the learning of their own topics, and thereby equally to promote language development; they may even, as the Bullock Report suggests they should, come to accept a share of responsibility for that development. And in any case 'language development' can never be the prime organising principle of a subject if it is also believed that the attempts, conducted in language, to understand the world need to be genuine ones. There have to be other grounds for selecting content and materials.

Despite the explanations they have given, English teachers have often in fact had regard to other considerations than language in devising their programmes; they have chosen topics, for instance, because they seemed important. But the dominant ideology, that it's all really for the language, has nevertheless had its effects. When

English of the more 'progressive' kind has been unsatisfactory it has often been precisely because content has been employed for the sake of language and not the other way round; 'stimulus material' has led to unanchored fantasising which has in no way been an attempt to get closer to reality. Assemblages of topics, particularly for the lower secondary years (Whales, Weddings, September 1939, Australia, Creation, Witches, Cats, Fishing . . .), linked by nothing except a hope that they will stimulate language, induce the same sort of numbness and disorientation as watching a whole evening's television or reading a colour supplement from cover to cover; the important is introduced along with the lightweight, the intimate with the macrocosmic, the near-to-home with the far-away; there are no bearings; issues are trivialised. If American Indians have to come up in the slot previously occupied by Eccentric People I Know and Fairgrounds, they were better not appearing at all; serious topics deserve to be introduced in a context in which the first concern is that children should seriously get to know about them.

Some common approaches at 14—16 are weakened in a similar way by the primacy given to certain uses of language over considerations of real understanding. Topics (such as the family, authority, old age, race and war) are often undertaken which may also be dealt with by other departments — social studies, humanities, RE, even geography and environmental science. The strength of the English approach at its best has been the way students have been encouraged to make their own relationships with the topic and to articulate, amplify and develop their personal responses to the issues. The weakness, however, as compared with, say, the social studies treatment, has been an insufficient regard for the need to know something about the topic. Students doing English projects who get involved for more than a brief period in acquiring and noting the facts about a topic make their teachers uneasy, although a full understanding may call for this. Relief is felt when the student switches to writing a poem or expressing his own views and responses.

Thus there is no alternative to taking the content of English seriously; and this implies, amongst other things, giving each topic the treatment it appears to call for on its own merits, irrespective of whether some of the activities go outside what we feel to be 'English'. English teachers have, de facto, taken responsibility for introducing their students to certain important aspects of the world, creating by their practice a job description for English that goes far beyond mere concern for language. Indeed, if the special language responsibility were taken from English and distributed across the subjects, and only literature (and perhaps the study of language as a phenomenon) were left to it, the loss which would be felt most seriously would be that of the distinctive *content* of English. English teachers simply need now to acknowledge openly what they already in a sense know, that they are teachers not only of language but of certain sorts of knowledge; and then to look rationally and openly at this knowledge as a valid component of the school curriculum.

We have now come, rather too easily it may seem, to the beginnings of a common rationale for English and the other subjects. Language is, or ought to be, the concern of all of them; all promote learning and knowing — and not just 'knowing how to' but knowledge about the world. But now we must register that the sort of knowledge that English leads to seems to be of a different kind from the sort acquired in, say, history; and that a 'topic' in English is not the same as a 'topic' in science. We need to look more closely at the nature of the content of English.

If we look at the actual matter that gets handled in English — the specific ideas, facts, references to the world and so on, the detailed substance of what is talked about — one feature is very striking, that a large proportion of it has come into the classroom with the students rather than the teacher. The knowledge which is in play in the other lessons has been fed into the situation for the most part by the teacher, either directly or through books and other aids. It comes to the student already pre-selected and pre-structured in a way designed to lead to a particular sort of learning. In English, on the other hand, the teacher may lay down a topic and may introduce material, but the business of the lesson will typically be the relating of these to what the students already know and feel and think; the emphasis will often be heavily on what the students do with material which is already in a sense in their heads. This is knowledge which has come into their possession not as a result of a teacher's intention that it should but simply as a result of being around in the world. The items have come to them piecemeal, randomly and in an unplanned way out of their encounters with reality. These encounters include experiences of the physical world, things people have said, ideas, television, books, previous lessons, their own feelings — by no means the one homogeneous type of data that a term like 'direct experience' might suggest.

This, then, is what is distinctive about the content of English. Although English may well have introduced into the curriculum certain important topics which would not have got there under the programmes of the other subjects, it is not the topic-list that gives

English its identity, but the sort of knowledge that is involved *within* the topics. English is about working on the knowledge we have acquired from the unsystematic processes of living, about giving expression to it and making it into a firmer and more conscious kind of knowledge. This is done through language, expressive and informal language in the first place, and eventually language akin to that of literature. Our students work through language on their own knowledge, and also gain access to other people's knowledge by way of their language, that is, through literature; we learn from literature in something like the way we do from working over our own experience.

The fact that it is literature that provides the model for the expression of knowledge in English brings us to another of the distinctive features of that knowledge. A chemistry teacher embarking on a topic with a class will usually be able to specify what the detailed content of the work will be and what learning is expected to result. For the English teacher, the detailed content, since a large part of it will come from the students, is unpredictable, and so therefore is the resulting learning. But quite apart from the unpredictability, even if English teachers wanted to specify the knowledge they hoped would result, they would be unable to. The sort of knowledge that is involved is not specifiable. That is why there are no English textbooks — in the sense of books which lay out the knowledge which the subject is centrally about. Other teachers can give a statement of what they want the students to know: the task then is, in a sense, to make that statement into a psychological awareness in the student. But what students end up knowing, as a result of their English work, about, say, people's motivations could never be set out as a series of propositions; instead, it would have to be revealed by the way, for instance, they handle characters in their stories. The knowledge can only be displayed by being brought to bear on particular real or imagined situations — as happens in literature.

Thus the knowledge which is handled in English is of a different kind from that which is explicitly taught in the other subjects and enshrined in their formulas, facts and texts. At this point we might conclude that here at last we have located an irreducible difference — until we note that the disciplines also contain another sort of knowledge.

Consider a zoologist who has made a study of a species of river fish. She will have knowledge about this fish derived from her reading, and will have added more knowledge from her own researches, some of which she intends to publish. But she will also know, as a result of living with the fish for a long time, such things as the bit of river they are likely to dart to next, how they will react when a shadow falls across the stream, and when the shoal do not feel at ease. This is knowledge too, but knowledge which she could not publish, not at any rate in the same form as the other; she could not express it as a series of facts and generalisations.

Unlike her formal zoological knowledge, this knowledge may well be shared with non-specialists — with, for instance, an observant boy who lives near the river and likes watching the fish. Perhaps we could call it 'pre-zoological' knowledge, and we might note that the boy who has it will have a good start if he wants to be a zoologist. In the same way children have sets of awarenesses which could be described as 'pre-psychological', 'pre-sociological' and so on.

This is the sort of knowledge that English is concerned with: knowledge at a stage before it can be expressed in explicit generalisations. In fact, the boy we have imagined might very well find himself writing about the fish in his English lesson, going back into what he knows and trying to give expression to it. What he writes will almost certainly be unlike a passage from a zoology book. More likely it will proceed by describing one particular shoal on one particular occasion, probably an imagined one, because only in that sort of way — through the presentation of some specific reality — can that sort of knowledge be expressed. The zoologist too, if she wanted to communicate that aspect of her knowledge, would have to write in that way.

English at its best recognises the validity of the knowledge that students bring to school with them, and provides means of expression — from informal conversation to consciously constructed poetic writings — which allow it to be considered and made more of. Much of this knowledge falls within the fields of other school subjects — for instance, children's knowledge of nature. Yet the other subjects tend to ignore this 'pre-disciplinary' knowledge and start from the assumption that the students know nothing, or nothing that is 'real knowledge' — even though adult practitioners could not practise their disciplines without these unspecifiable awarenesses and sensitivities. Some good primary schools manage to bring both sorts of knowledge together, enabling the children's own experience to be illuminated by the public knowledge in books. In such schools, when two ten-year-olds dissect a rotten log they have brought into school and write about it, it is not asked whether that is English or science. But in the secondary school English teachers tend to steer clear of rotten logs, and of the whole exciting business of seriously observing natural processes, because they feel they would be trespassing on the territory of science, while in science, although logs may be dissected and the discoveries written about, the type of writing typically sanctioned denies expression to nine-tenths of the experience — and certainly runs no risk of being mistaken for English. It is good that a passage from Leonardo's notebooks analysing a bird's flight appears in an English anthology, but one suspects that English teachers will generally feel inhibited from using it while science teachers, although the topic is within their field, will reject that sort of presentation of it.

Thus the kind of knowledge which is promoted by English is not, as first appears, peculiar to it but is common to all the disciplines; the way the disciplines are taught, however, tends to conceal this underlying similarity. The separation in the secondary school curriculum of the scientific (in the broad sense) from the personal and intuitive ways of knowing fails to reflect the psychological realities of most of the students under 16 that I have known. It does not correspond to any achieved differentiation in their thinking; few of them have come to regard objectivity and the establishment of impersonal truth as values in themselves. Arrival at that stage appears indeed to be hindered by teaching approaches which insist on the outward forms of objectivity and which exclude the larger part of the child's response.

Enough has been said to show why English has come to be a unique phenomenon in education. Under the guise of just another curriculum subject, it has come to enact nothing less than a different model of education: knowledge to be made, not given; knowledge comprising more than can be discursively stated; learning as a diverse range of processes, including affective ones; educational processes to be embarked on with outcomes unpredictable; students' perceptions, experiences, imaginings and unsystematically acquired knowledge admitted as legitimate curricular content. It is no wonder that English teachers, operating within a single subject space, have sometimes felt a sense of constriction.

It is a fruitless exercise to try to construct an account of English which will locate it rationally in terms of the overall aims of the curriculum. The key insights of the model of education it now embryonically realises need to be built into the practice of the other subjects. Then the common ground will be a fact. When this happens, and when restrictions deriving from institutional divisions which do not reflect the realities of learning are removed, English may or may not continue to exist as a distinct institution; certainly the label 'English' can suggest the wrong principle of organisation.

What is needed now is to identify the vital elements at present contributed by English and the other subjects and to devise arrangements under which they may all be provided for. The following seem to be some of the essential considerations; in effect they provide the agenda for the rest of this book:-

Certain *topics* seem to merit inclusion in the curriculum. Some justify their presence because they are central to a discipline or aptly exemplify its concepts and procedures. Others are important for students to experience for different reasons, social, political and personal; in this category will come some of the topics English has introduced into the curriculum.

Literature has a place in its own right (irrespective of any 'topics' it may contribute to).

For topics to be adequately learnt, or learnt about, or learnt within, they need to be actively handled by students in their own *language*. This is the process that also leads to competence in language, and is the one whereby competence needs to be developed. It makes sense that those who take responsibility for the topics should consciously seek to promote the best language experience at the same time. This is the meaning of language across the curriculum. (The implications of this argument, with particular reference to writing practice, will be taken up in Chapter 2.)

Whenever these processes are allowed to take place, what ends up being learnt is to some extent *unpredictable*. (It always was in any case: getting the knowledge was never just a matter of internalising the statements of the knowledge.) This needs to be accepted in all subjects as it now is in the best English practice; teaching can never be completely programmatic; we always have to improvise on the run, building on the diverse constructions that students make for themselves out of what is given them.

In all the disciplines there is a *personal and unstateable knowledge* which needs to be worked on as well as the publicly formulated sort. Those who deal with the discipline should also recognise and allow expression to the 'pre-disciplinary' awarenesses that students bring to school with them. Before we ever meet those diagrams of arteries and veins, we all know things about blood which we need to sort out for ourselves and bring into line with the new insights biology gives us. And we acquire some knowledge which can only be expressed and made substantial by the kinds of talk and writing which have hitherto been too exclusively associated with English.

All topics should receive the *full range of treatment* that they demand, with no holds barred either on the side of factual inquiry or of personal response. The full repertoire of educational processes should be available to be deployed on any topic.

However a particular topic has got onto the agenda for teacher and class, the detailed content of the proceedings needs to be *determinable by students* as well as teacher; they need to be able to put their questions, preoccupations and knowledge into the pool of what gets dealt with. (Chapter 3 in particular will pursue this point.)

2 The uses of writing

In examining the use of language in the other subjects we need to draw, as I have suggested, on English teachers' experience, interpreting it, however, from the point of view of a primary concern with understanding rather than with language. Writing is the activity in which the results of such an examination will show up most distinctively and I therefore make it the theme of this chapter. The procedure must be to specify the sort of educational needs which writing might fulfil and to discover the conditions and contexts which would enable it to perform those functions.

To begin with a basic question. When students are learning about a new area of knowledge, what is the point of their writing anything? It has been the normal school practice for any new piece of learning to be accompanied by writing, and yet a typical adult who has become interested in a subject and is engaged in finding out more about it, outside the context of formal educational study, will not automatically turn to writing as an essential aid; many people simply read books from the library and derive knowledge adequate to their purposes from that activity alone; or they seek out others with the same interest and talk to them.

Here is a piece of school writing:

Los Angeles has a population of seven million, the city is divided into 47 townships. It is about six times bigger than greater London. There is one car for every two people so there is a terrific traffic problem, there is 450 miles of motor way some with ten lanes going the same way. Just out side Los Angeles is hollywood where every actor wants to go and become a star. Los Angeles's main industries is aircraft. They also make all their own materials for the wheels, metals etc. In Los Angeles the buses only work in the morning and evening rush hours, because so many people have cars. It is the home of the Great Lockheed Company, Santa Barbara just out side Los Angeles. The climate is hot all the year round, it only rains about two weeks a year, so it attracts a lot of visitors in winter. But the sky is not blue because of all the exhaust fumes caused by all the cars, there is a continuous haze over the city, the Americans call it smog.

Paul, a 12-year-old boy, wrote this in the second half of a geography lesson. During the first part the teacher had talked, in an interesting way, about Los Angeles, using the blackboard to jot down a few facts and names, and then had asked the class to write their account of Los Angeles. Most teachers will recognise the writing that resulted as a familiar type, and the procedure as a common and accepted one.

The statements in Paul's account are more or less true. The teacher would have been justified in thinking that something of what he had said had got over. But it is worth noting also that the facts are not presented in a coherent order: three sentences (the first two are divided by a comma) about the size, two (punctuated as one) about cars, one about Hollywood; then two about the aircraft industry, another relating to cars, and a further one about the aircraft industry — but to recognise it as such you need to know that Lockheed make aircraft, for we are not told this; climate; then a final point relating climate to cars.

To many of us, this way of organising our lessons, with this sort of provision for a writing task in Part 2, comes as second nature and we do not think very hard or often about the educational theory the practice expresses. But if we were pressed, our justification would probably be in these terms:

— Having to write it down forces the students to go over the information again in their heads; this second exposure will help them to remember it, and there may also be something about the physical business of writing that aids the memory — the fact associated with the particular pattern on the page, perhaps.
— The student also has to get the knowledge organised into some sort of shape in order to write it down.
— It provides a convenient way for the teacher to monitor what has been learnt.

This seems like a reasonable case.

It is a feature, however, of writing that arises out of this kind of educational context that it does not notably show evidence of any particular intelligence or qualities of mind which the writer may possess: one student's work is very like another's. It is as if, when what is required is the taking in of information, there is little to be intelligent about. The justification for this sort of rehearsal of a set of facts would be that it is simply a means of taking possession of them, and that this part of the process does not call for intelligent thought.

It is certainly true that intelligence and skill come into the process at the point when knowledge is mobilised in new contexts; it is also noteworthy that most teaching does little to develop that ability. But perhaps there are also more intelligent and less intelligent ways of receiving the knowledge in the first place. Perhaps the use you can make of knowledge later depends partly on what you do with it when you first encounter it.

Anecdotal evidence may give us a way in. We all know good talkers who not only can express themselves well but who also have things to say on a wide variety of issues and are worth listening to for the interpretations they put on almost anything that comes up. One way of characterising their ability is to say that they are exceptionally able to make use of the knowledge they have acquired from different sources in the course of their living — knowledge from direct experience, from reading, from school, from conversation and from the media. Whatever the topic is, they can find something relevant which will throw light on it or make it look different, and the pieces of illuminating knowledge or thinking may come from the most disparate origins. They have efficient retrieval systems, cross-indexed under a very large number of headings.

When I look for what is different about the way such people operate, my impression is that they are special in the way they deal with new knowledge. Watching television, for instance, they tend to comment on the information as it arrives, rather than to receive it in silence — drawing comparisons, expressing surprise, speculating on implications, formulating hypotheses — provided there is someone else in the room, that is. If a second person arrives on the scene only half way through, or afterwards, the viewer will produce the commentary then, in an instantly turned-on flow, as if the information has already somehow been composed into a near-verbal mode ready for utterance. Thus the processes that appear to be characteristic of these individuals' eventual *use* of information in contexts that arise, also typify their initial *reception* of it. New knowledge is immediately related to other experience.

These efficient 'natural learners' also seem, to a greater extent than the rest of us, to have general views. They exhibit not only a rich fund of particular knowledge and ideas but also an integrated overall outlook towards whole aspects of reality, in such a way that one feels they have come, perhaps not explicitly, to some large conclusions about the world, which give a distinctive colour to all their attitudes. It is as if the habit of asking the 'so what?' question about everything has led to the continual consideration of larger and larger issues and the synthesising and integration of broad areas of experience. This process, which occurs spontaneously in some people, could possibly be promoted in school in far more people. Perhaps writing could help; perhaps it could carry the functions of questioning and connection-making in relation to new knowledge, and of synthesising and integrating knowledge over wide areas.

We know that an active and questioning reception of new information can occur naturally in talk. But a it also happens in writing; there are letters and diaries which are full of a very obvious processing of whatever has recently impinged on the sensibility. Why can it not occur naturally in school writing? Or perhaps the question is better asked negatively in the first place: what at present is stopping it happening?

The categories for classifying writing which were developed by the Schools Council Writing Research are a useful tool here.* They enable us to locate a piece of writing on a grid according to two dimensions, in relation to other pieces of writing. One beauty of such grids is that they suggest types which have not been found but could theoretically exist; then we can, if we wish, set about bringing them into existence. Two dimensions of classification were developed in detail, those of Function and Audience. The functions of writing, in this sense, are not simply the purposes for which it is in fact used but are socially recognised types of writing associated with types of purposes.

If we apply this model to Paul's piece on Los Angeles, it appears to fall into the informative function. It looks like the type of writing you get when a writer is concerned to make available to a reader a set of facts about a topic. Paul imitates what informative writers — probably textbook writers — do. But a peculiar feature of Paul's writing soon becomes apparent. A type of writing which has been developed to perform a particular function — informing — is being used not for that function but for a quite different one: for it is no part of the student's intention here to inform anyone of anything. No-one's ignorance is to be alleviated by Paul's account. So far from that being the case, the person who will read it — the teacher — is the one in the whole world who is least in need of being given this information, since he was the immediate source of it. If the point of the writing was to aid the grasping of the information and to provide the teacher with evidence of understanding, the question suggests itself, Why not use a form specifically adapted to those purposes instead of one which was intended for completely different ones?

The conventional answer is that requiring students to write as if they were informing others is actually the best way to help them to

*Britton J. et al, *The development of writing abilities 11–18,* Macmillan, 1975

make sense of the knowledge. But the writing that results, while it may aid factual recall, manifestly does not do much for those processes of questioning and making connections that I indicated might be essential if the information is later to be usable. Here there is little scope for anything but facts, or indeed for the facts in more or less the form they were given in. Moreover, this use of writing is not even an adequate means of testing since, while it reveals that certain facts have been recollected, it does not show what misunderstandings and delusions lie around and just outside the area specifically dealt with.

It is unlikely, after all, that Paul was seeking to provide the teacher with *true* information about the state of his knowledge — gaps and all: the unspoken aim in this game is to satisfy the teacher that you know it, whether you actually do or not. Well below the surface and at a level where few teachers would be conscious of it, the assumption behind this practice is that students will not willingly seek to improve their knowledge, so that devices have to be found to force them into it and to show up the gaps they will naturally try to conceal. Clearly, such procedures will be unlikely to produce learning to compare with that of the motivated and spontaneous 'natural learners' we referred to earlier.

The second dimension of classification in the Writing Research model is Sense of Audience: the way a message is written will vary according to the type of recipient it is intended for. In this respect too we find a pretence operating in the Los Angeles and similar pieces. The writer in no way acknowledges the actual relationship obtaining between himself and his reader, the teacher. Instead, he adopts certain outward characteristics of a writer whose work was destined for a general readership. Paul pretends to be addressing an audience who will not in fact read his work; and he pretends to be someone other than who he is , in that he plays the role of the fully informed expert in a position to teach others about Los Angeles. Manifestly, there is little scope in such a contrived performance for him to express any of his own tentative thoughts, reactions and puzzlements.

Not surprisingly, most students do not do well with this type of writing. Keeping up the pretence of writing for an imaginary audience for an imaginary purpose in an imaginary persona presents unnecessary additional problems to a student faced with mastering a new body of knowledge. Younger students' experience of using language, almost all of it, has been of communication between particular, known people. So the task the child is faced with must feel something like talking in an empty room, to nobody — and under observation from a one-way mirror.

Some students are able to manage something even under these constrained circumstances, and even to enjoy the game, pleasurably anticipating the teacher's reaction to their pretend public communication. But it is worth noting that such success comes not from the students' achieving the implicit requirements of the task but from their discovery of a successful way round it, in finding a real and personal addressee to hold in mind while writing rather than in developing an adequate concept of a public audience.

An alternative is possible: to see writing as an option we can take up for a variety of purposes, and to specify the type of writing which will best achieve the needs of the moment. We can control the process, rather than simply submit to its irrational demands.

One can work out in general terms the requirements for a type of writing which would give learners the opportunity to do something for themselves with the knowledge they were being presented with. Such writing would depend on a context in which students were taken seriously as learners with some stake in the business of learning; its form would not be dictated by the need to test them. The writers would have to be able to be themselves, and to talk in a natural way to whoever really was to be the reader. Any pretence should be conscious role-playing deliberately assumed. Above all, the child should be able to feel at ease with the form of the writing and the relationship it expressed. Coming out with thoughts and ideas of your own entails the risk of making a fool of yourself, as does admitting to difficulty and ignorance; the student must therefore feel confident that the teacher will read as a sympathetic helper and not as a judge and marker.

When writing like this ceases to be a mere theoretical possibility and begins to occur in our students' exercise books as a result of changes in our practice, its appearance can at first be disturbing. Its informality and lack of clear structure, and the way that personal responses, emotions and even humour get mixed up with the information, upset our ideas of what school learning should look like. But learning never was — except in psychology books and education lectures — the precise, white-coated, cleanly cognitive affair we would half like it to be. We have learnt to think of our students' observation of the internal structure of the dogfish as the real substance of their dealings with it, and to dismiss their feelings of nausea or excitement at cutting into the flesh and smelling its smell as mere 'noise'. Yet the intellectual apprehension of a reality does not come on its own. The learner is a whole person and responds with all of a person's faculties and sensitivities. The intellectual grasp may actually be keenest when the other, non-cognitive sorts of attention are most aroused. Even if cognitive understanding is the outcome we are ultimately concerned to promote, we nevertheless need, in the early stages at least, to be hospitable to the entire response. This comes in one global form and not as a collection of separable expressions, and if we attempt to exclude the 'irrelevant' aspects we will almost certainly kill off the part we want as well.

We have considered one piece written in response to new knowledge. Here is another:

China is a large overcrowded country in Eastern Asia that inhabits a $\frac{1}{4}$ of the population in less than $\frac{1}{8}$ of the area but this country is not like you may think it may be but it is one of the most organised states in the world. All that everybody thinks about is "We are doing it for the People's Republic just like Chairman Mao says." It may in one way be a backward country but in many others it is the most industrialist country in the world. Everything done is done in a simple way. If a rock has to be moved a man in a red monkey suit will say, "You two move it" and they will not get a lorry or a tractor but sling a piece of rope round it, put a piece of wood through, pick it up and take it to where it should be. No problem of a fuel crisis, all that's needed to keep these going is a handful of rice a day. That's how things work in this most happy and honourable of countries. A little man in a red suit with a yellow face seems to be everywhere telling you what to do, where to go, how to get there like a mini information bureau. All those people believe in an ideal, work for an ideal and live for an ideal, a better land, a better home, the chance of a better race, the fair and promised land, the essence of all communism, all good communism at least. This is a land where selfishness is a dirty word. Nobody must think of China just like a poor man's Russia.

This recalls those qualities of the 'natural learner' and good talker which I spoke of earlier. The information (in this case from a film shown in the lesson) is immediately seized on and ascribed a significance; the student (Tony, aged 15) wastes no time in putting the new knowledge to a use of his own, which is to arrive at a rapid judgment of China. What he is saying here is, this is what China represents for me. The specific bits of information act as evidence for his general implicit assertion that China is such-and-such a sort of place. The general idea provides Tony with the criteria for what to include and what to miss out, and what weight to give to each part.

This is not to say that the piece is highly organised, but it is effective and economical in the same way as the speech of a person with a clear point of view.

I am not suggesting that this piece represents a satisfactory *final* outcome of a piece of learning: merely that it makes a hopeful starting point. At least we can feel confident that the information recorded here has been securely 'learnt' and will stay with Tony for some time. The fact that he is now thinking about the topic and has arrived at a provisional interpretation means that it will be easy to get him to consider further evidence and other interpretations; he will have a stake in looking seriously at them since they will affect the construction he has made.

This piece is not simply and objectively about China; rather, it is about 'China and me'. In this it is like 'English writing'. We often find when we open up the writing channels and enable students to say whatever they feel a need to say about a new topic that what they need to say turns out to be not only observations on the, as it were, 'internal' details of the topic but reactions to encountering the topic as a whole. It seems there is a need for students to answer for themselves questions like: 'How do I place me-doing-this in my total idea of myself? What do I make of the experience of being here and engaged in this activity?' Until one sees this happening in the writing one may not realise there is a need for it; we expect students immediately to become absorbed in a new topic, whereas in fact there sometimes needs to be a definite stage in which they get into a relationship with it.

There has to be an explanation why Tony wrote this way about China and Paul wrote the other way about Los Angeles. There are several differences in the two situations. Tony actually was in an English lesson, not a geography lesson: the film had been hired for a course on China but it was decided to show it in addition to an English group. So different expectations about the type and function of writing were operating. Secondly, Tony wrote this off his own bat, without being asked. The group was not instructed to write about the film but Tony decided to because he felt he had something to say. So he was not in the position of being told to say something and having to cook up something to say, which leads so commonly to the type of writing which the Writing Research informally dubbed 'random information retrieval'. Lastly, although the writing is not ostensibly addressed to anyone in particular, it is probably relevant that he and I got on exceptionally well and he could feel sure that I would enjoy his effort.

We tend to expect writing to be 'special' in a way that we don't expect of talk. If a child makes an observation in talk we are satisfied if it is useful and helpful. Is there not a place for a sort of writing which claims to do no more than a spoken comment may and can be accepted simply as a small but probably useful formulation? The other pieces I am going on to quote should be looked at from that point of view: that is, they show not what surprising things can be achieved but simply what that writing looks and smells like which assists the everyday function of thinking and talking on paper, with a supportive audience in mind, about new knowledge and ideas.

It is helpful to think of this writing in terms of another of the Writing Research Function categories, not the informative but the expressive. Most of our everyday talk is in this function. Although 'expressive' suggests that we use it to display our feelings, which we do, we also give information, tell stories and do many other things: it is an unspecialised and mixed use of language which comes easily to us in relaxed communicative situations and which we naturally resort to when we need to 'think aloud'. Its educational relevance in view of the requirements we have noted for our sought-after language for learning will be quite clear.

Tony's China piece occurred without being planned for by the teacher. In the humanities department I worked in, we deliberately set about creating a writing channel which students could use in an informal and relaxed way, and the idea of log books suggested itself. The way we explained the log book to students was that it was *at minimum* a record of what they had been doing, useful to us because there was often a variety of activities going on in the group, including ephemeral ones like discussion and film-viewing which would not otherwise get recorded; but beyond that it could, if the students wished, be a space in which they could think aloud on paper and write to their teacher in any way they chose. The teachers would write back and a correspondence could develop.

When we first introduced logs, such was the strength of traditional expectations about school writing that it was hard to get students to accept that they could actually write to their teacher directly and not just in the guise of addressing some imaginary public. Thus in the early days of a school year (14 October) Carl (13), writing to me (he knew very well there was to be no other reader), put (my italics)

Mr Medway was wrong when he said that I had been watching Ice Station Zebra. I'd been watching a million dollar brain. This morning I have been writing my thoughts on two topics. The first one was what would happen if oil went up to £2.50 a gallon and the second was what would happen if oil went down to 50p a gallon. If any should come true I would prefer the first one, would you *who ever is going to read this?*

By 13 January his log book was fulfilling more of the role we had intended. In this entry he refers to a passage from *The teachings of Don Juan* by Carlos Castaneda:

The thing that you read to us on Monday, I thought it was very interesting but somehow I don't think it could be true. Some parts could be true but the parts I think are not true are:- Meeting the spirits in the mountains, going through the door and coming out somewhere else. But if the things are true why don't scientists go looking for them. And if it is all true it proves that the so called red Indian isn't so primitive after all. Do you agree with me? And also there could be a lot to learn from them. And if all the other primitive peoples know things like this it could open up a whole new science or range of studies. And I think that I might want to look into what the man's saying a little bit more. Although I think it can't be true I have got a feeling it could be true. Do you think so?

It is useful, to claim nothing more, that students should be able to note down questions, uncertainties and possibilities as they reflect in an unpressured and unhurried way (there's the difference from classroom talk) on the new experience they have been exposed to. It enables the teacher to know which lines could be pursued to most advantage with particular students, but it also helps the students if they consciously identify points of interest or concern: they are opening files which can be taken up and worked on in the future. We could have said about our 'good talkers' that they have files already building up on many topics and are constantly prepared to open new ones.

What emerged as probably the prime function of the log books was the making of an overall response. They were not normally used as vehicles for going systematically over the detail of the topic. The writing of Joanne (13) was a good example. On one occasion I had given her an extract to read about an anthropologist who was accepted by an Amazonian tribe only after a long period in which he was regarded as an animal; the piece describes many features of this experience and of the Indians' way of life, attitudes to dreams, special interest in pottery and so on, most of which Joanne does not pick up, choosing instead to use the evidence of the extract towards conclusions of her own:

Anthropologist in the Xingu

It is a very fascinating story, and I think he is lucky to be able to tell
it. They could easily not have accepted him, and left him to die. It
was very exciting for him I expect. I would like to be him, the
Waura tribe are very interesting. The Waura tribe know a lot about
medicines and stuff which we don't. We are ruled by machines, they
do everything for us. But the Waura are opposite to us, they have to
get their own food. And make everything which they use. They
don't use money, so they don't fight over it. They seem to enjoy life
a lot without using machines, they eat all different things as well. If
you stayed there for a very long time you might not want to go back
to civilisation. I think it would be good if people went there to live
for a year, they would appreciate life better. And might even find it
fun. The Waura tribe must be clever to keep alive. Because if most
of us went and tried to live like them, not many people would keep
alive.

Between the naive expressive of the young writer and the disciplined
communication of developed informative discourse lies a wider range
of intermediate posibilities than is generally recognised. It is therefore
quite possible for students to preserve their sense of their own voice
and of their personal involvement with their subject matter as they
gradually take on more demanding forms. Organisation and
structure are important also to the poetic function of language as in
stories, plays and poems, and there can be the same gradual
progression towards mature forms in these kinds of writing. A few
examples will indicate the variety of forms which can be drawn on;
others will be described in later chapters.

Dramatic presentations of knowledge afford a means whereby
students can at the same time feel they are offering something unique
and interesting to an audience and work over the knowledge in ways
that lead to a fuller grasp of it. Moreover they contain the possibility
of different degrees of organisation of the material, depending on how
far the writer attempts or is able to meet the criteria of a mature
poetic production: thus the writer can develop within the same sort of
form out of the expressive and into more consciously constructed
communication.

The following piece, by Simon (11), is about *Treasure Island*. The
teacher's idea in setting the assignment was to enable the students to
review the story so far and assess how much had happened; but it also
enabled each student to make an interesting presentation of his or her
own.

That night in bed, Jim Hawkins lies awake thinking over how his life has changed since the coming of the captain.

Ah it's a relief to feel safe in bed after all thats happened. How long has it been since I could lie in bed without a worry. It's so long ago that I can't remember. But it all comes back to me now. The day the captain came, the captain himself with his sea going songs and glasses of rum every ten minutes and the language he used after he'd had one or two. Then there was the excitement of feeling impotent and scared as the captain told me why he really was here and why he kept to himself and the salary he paid me was a lot. I think I've got about 15 shillings. Let's see now, he paid me a shilling a month and he stayed just over one and a half years. He started paying me after two months and that makes it 16 shillings exactly. Then theres the episode of Black Dog. Horrid fellow tap-tapping along the street with no eyes asking for money and I'll never forget the shock of when he turned round grabbed me and asked for Billy Bones, yes that will always stay in my mind, and of course two deaths in less than a week. My father and the captain both of which I was very close to and yet a third death this time someone I hated. This was Black Dog or Pew as his ship mates called him. This adventure I shall not forget and yet it is just beginning.

A more deliberate construction with a concern for the shape of the reader's experience, and at the same time a detailed presentation of a piece of history — thus, communication for others: learning for oneself — is shown in a piece by Derek (13) entitled

Committee of Inquiry into Colliery disaster, January 10th 1816. The evidence of John Smith, miner, age 30

Questioner	Could you tell us in your own words where you were half past one on January 10th?
John Smith	Ad just finished me snap. I wa walking down to face 2 to start work.
Questioner	Did you smell anything different?
John Smith	No, nowt. An we had them new Davy lamps and that wa all reit.
Questioner	What were you doing on face 2?
John Smith	We wa making some new piller a coal.
Questioner	Why were you doing that?
John Smith	Well that's ow we old roof up by leavin piller o uncut coal.

Questioner	Then what happened?
John Smith	Well all o' a sudden a crack came over us heads. I shouts to me mates "come on get out".
Questioner	Did everyone get out?
John Smith	Did they eck. About 10 of us got out and 15 got copt. All roof came in just where we'd made new pillers.
Questioner	After the roof had stopped coming in what happened?
John Smith	We told two o' men to go back an' tell gaffer. The were ponies an women an kids trapped. We tried to find bodies.
Questioner	When you had dug the bodies out how were they?
John Smith	There wa blood an muck everywhere. 14 on em were dead an our Joey brock is back.
Questioner	Did you help them briing the bodies up to the top?
John Smith	Yes. We carried em for over a mile till we came to shaft.
Questioner	You say you didn't smell gas. You don't think it was an explosion?
John Smith	No, bodies wont burnt.
Questioner	Do you think that someone had cut the piller too thin?
John Smith	Yes.
Questioner	Have you anything more to say?
John Smith	No.
Questioner	Thank you. You may go now. Send in the next one please.

In the final example of this chapter we can see the beginnings of the transition from expressive ('getting it down' for oneself) to informative (organising it for someone else); perhaps from English to sociology. It suggests one way in which English needs to be organically related to the other parts of the humanities curriculum. Garry (14) was one of a small group who did a study of York Railway Station. His report is written in sections, corresponding to those in which the study was carried out. Some of these are more markedly related to the expressive narrative associated with English, others to more impersonal reporting. Here are four of the sections:

Buffet

We went out of the station for our dinner but went into the buffet for a cup of coffee with cream on. As I drank the coffee through the cream I gazed around watching different people. Four tables away from us there was four businessmen.

One was a very cocky looking man because he looked at me as if to say, I'm it, you're rubbish. I just gave him a dirty look.

There were one with a normal look and a big fat one that just kept laughing at me. The fourth man was a clever looking man and very stern and stiffly built. All he did was turn round and discuss something with the 3 women on the next table. They were about of his class . . .

Movement

I stood on the crossing bridge and watched the movement of the people. I found most people walked with shoulders forwards facing the floor and moving slow. Those who were carrying bags would every so often drop their bags put both hands on back and push body forwards. Then there were others who thought they were it who walked stiff and straight thinking they owned the place. Some would walk slow thinking then stop and walk back where they come from but roughly they all walked in the same direction like swarms of ants.

Surfaces

The station bricks were very interesting. They were very smooth and a nice shadey effect and when I got near they had small holes in. When I rubbed my hand over a few dust fell which indicated they had been made from a sandy mixture.

Then I went over to touch a wagon wheel. They were full of thick dirty grease that you could have scraped off and parts of them were rough with rust which had a cutting feeling when gently rubbed.

Behaviour

A station makes people behave in many different ways
Worried
Happy
Move quick
Searching for the right platform
Looking around
following other people to see where they go
dashing about
Asking porters for the right platform
Darting first in one direction then in the next

Looking for the right trains when they pull in
but those that use the station just get their ticket find
the right platform and wait for the train.

It is along this sort of route that one would expect to bring students to
mastery of the informative function in the expository essay, the
research report and similar forms, by maintaining the writers' sense
of saying something in their own right while increasing their
awareness of the needs of a wide and unknown potential audience.
What these examples suggest is that it is crucial that learners should
feel themselves to be basically in charge of their own learning, makers
as well as learners, and contributors as well as receivers. The practical
implications of this need are far-reaching and will be taken up in the
next chapter.

3 Autonomy and the working-class freelance

Implied throughout the previous chapter was the suggestion that if students are to write in ways that will help them learn they need to have a say over what to write and when. If the most useful writing arises out of a sense of having something to communicate, only the writer knows when he is in this position and we cannot pretend to be in full control of the timing or the content of the process; and in fact the writing we see which most clearly represents new learning often turns out to have originated with a student's and not a teacher's decision; or at least when it was open to the writer to take his own line on the topic. This opportunity is necessary even when the topic is factual and when the facts are the same for everyone and have been gone over by generations of learners in the past: even here the student needs to be in a position to make a real communication and a real contribution, to offer something to a reader, through an individual interpretation or use of the facts, which could not have been got from somewhere else (and especially from a textbook). So success depends on resources being brought into play which are under the students' control and not ours. Speculative and reflective activity, imagining and questioning, cannot simply be programmed into our lesson plans to appear at particular times and on our terms.

Thus in taking account of the realities of the writing process in the ways we organise our classroom, we inescapably find ourselves involved with the notion of student autonomy. But this is in any case where we need to be, on other grounds too. Our ideas of what we should be trying to do come to us from different sources, but some are almost forced on us by characteristics we find in our students. During the notorious 'Three Day Week'* of 1974 I floated the idea to a group of students who were shortly to leave school that a working week of three days would have a lot to be said for it, provided that the same income would result as from five days. Most of them strongly

*Because of a coalminers' strike the Heath government introduced electricity rationing so that industry was supplied with power for only three days in each week, with the result that large numbers of workers were laid off for the remaining days.

disagreed, on the grounds that they would not have enough to do in the long periods unfilled by work. It struck me that an education (eleven years of it) which produced people who felt like that left something to be desired, and my conviction was strengthened that autonomy — being able to do things on one's own, and wanting to — needed to become a central aim of education. I was already acutely aware that the experience of many of our students was of being circulated from lesson to lesson without ever becoming personally engaged in what was going on, forgetting in the process all they ever knew about seeking their own ways to satisfy curiosities, interests and creative impulses. The personal search for understanding was undoubtedly still a potent underlying drive, but it had long ago got disconnected from the formal education process. Personal intention as the generator of activity, so predominant in the first five years of life, by 15 appeared to have abandoned the scene, at any rate during school hours — except in the pursuit of illicit peergroup satisfactions. So it seems to me to be an urgent need to restore personal purpose to the educational scene, and the requirements of the writing process merely confirm the necessity for a curriculum built around a degree of student autonomy.

Meanwhile, some of our adolescent students are already making it clear where they stand on this issue. In the whole of their attitude and behaviour they lay claim to autonomy, asserting unambiguously that it is they, not we, who will decide what they will and will not do. Generally, because this position has led to rejection of our prescribed curriculum and to disruptive behaviour, we have seen it as inimical to education, and have lived in a state of continuous warfare with it. But should we not see manifestations of autonomy, of whatever type, as hopeful signs of life which we ought to be able to work with? Our attitude to the intelligent and consciously anti-school working-class student is the real test of the adequacy of our educational philosophies.

I have known many such students, self-respecting individuals of both sexes who prized their independence above everything and would go along with me only to the extent that I 'sold' them the work as promising enjoyment. Their view of teachers as a group, of school and of conforming 'good students' was contemptuous; they were unmoved by the allurements of exam grades and 'better jobs'; as is often pointed out, they attached importance to the enjoyable texture of immediate experience, and especially to 'laughs'; but at the same time they held to some solid social values about such things as family, a worthwhile life, and the place of money in happiness. For me the essence of this whole position is expressed in the testimony of an ex-student of mine, Barry, who I talked to when he was 19 and working as a miner. It makes quite implausible the idea of any other basis for the education of this type of student than respect for their autonomy.

'I didn't like being pushed around when I was at school, mainly because I felt I was too old or felt I was a man or something. I didn't like bloody teachers just walking up, "You're going to do this, you're going to do that, and you must do this, that and t'other." You get all these stupid little creeps running round to do it. I used to think, Aw, bugger this, why should I do six pages full of writing when I could be flicking spit at somebody with my ruler?

I couldn't give a toss about school. I only went mainly because of t'humanities. You were t'main reason why I went there. I aren't being greasing or owt like that, but that's only reason why I went because it was something that I wanted to do. You didn't force nowt on me, not like t'rest of t'teachers — "You've *got* to do this and you've got to do homework." If a teacher says "You've *got* to do this", you know — I've *got* to do rock all, you know, I am it, you know, you're not telling me what to do. So you're sat down there pretending to write and really you're chalking away on t'bloody desk.

I think a teacher's a person that wants to put intelligence into someone like a bloody factory animal. I think the perfect teaching system would be to have kids there with built-in impulses to be sat in rows, take it all in, write it all down and remember it for ever. I mean they're trying to make them like ruddy little computers.

Teachers waint come true wi' you, never, and it's same at t'pit, bloody management'll never come true to you. They're allus behind t'bloody door planning summat behind your back, up to summat, they wain't tell you, there's always that doubtful feeling there, you know.

There were some that wanted to work all t'time and have a little bit of a laugh, them that wanted to work all t'time and have no laughs, and them that wanted to just have laughs all t'time. I don't know which category I was in — I wanted to have a laugh a lot of t'time, but I didn't want to take advantage of you, and I wanted to do summat what I wanted to do, you know, like reading the books that you gave me to read. If I wanted to do summat and them lot were messing around it were a bit hard. If I were with a load of intelligent gits and I wanted them to have a laugh, you couldn't do, you know. They were allus on about, "Oh, you're going to go down t'pit, I'm going to get a right good job, I'm going to be a mechanic" — this, that and t'other. Half of them's gone down t'pit now. They haven't had a laugh at school. Silly buggers that are doing mechanics, they ain't on half as much money as me, they're skint every week, they don't go up town, they don't get birds, they don't get nowt. You know, they've got this bloody dream: I've got to be successful, I've got to be successful, you know. Well, fucking hell, success, when you come to think about it, eh — bald, grey, you know, and you think, "Oh, I've worked myself up to this position," but you're too old to bloody use it, aren't you? They'll be skint when they're all young. When they get to t'money stage they're going to be too bloody old to use it, you know.

People in t'office, they never finish work. They do very little manual work. All it is is up here, and it's more or less automatic what they do then, so you may as well kick that in t'head cause they never finish their work. They may only work bloody five hours a day but it's still on their mind all t'time when they get home. They think, "What the bloody hell's going to happen tomorrow, you know. Have I done this right, have I done t'other right, I think I should do some overtime for nothing, boss, can I lick your bum for you," — you know, that kind of thing. Whereas me, I just go down t'pit, get that ripping shoved away, come out and I think, "Chuff t'pit, it ought to blow up." I wanted to have summat like a life where I could be content, you know. I think that were a big thing, that contentment. There were only me and my father at home, and I could go home any time I want whether he were in or not, you know, stick a record on, throw my clothes anywhere and lie down on t'settee, 'cause I can talk to my dad really well, talk to him about anything, birds, sex, booze, you name it. He's a smashing bloke, is my dad. He's a character and a half, him. I think he maybe influenced me a lot through my life, I don't know. But there must have been a lot there already — bloody rogue! Probably a lot of people call me a wrong un, you know, somebody who isn't normal — "you don't want to know him! you know, he's one of them kids that don't agree with us."

If we do get married, do have kids and that, we're going to be happy and content. We might never have any money but we're going to be happy with each other in what we've got, 'cause that's t'way it's always been in our family. Any member of our family can walk into t'pub or walk into t'house any time they want and get on like a house on fire — fall out one minute, have laughs with each other t'next, you know. That's t'way it goes. You can see that love and that in t'kids.

I've always thought of myself as somebody different. I've always thought to myself, well, I like what I am and chuff all t'rest. If them lot want to wear bloody tights, well let all t'lads wear tights, I'm going to carry on wearing what I want to wear. If I like any styles that come in I'll probably buy it, but otherwise I just stay as myself, last of the hippies kind of thing, you know.

Don't tread the trodden path, tread thi bloody own. Yes, that's t'way I seem to think. People say I'm going this road in life, that road in life. I ain't going any road in life. I'm doing what I want to, you know. It's not hard for me to follow any line 'cause I'm myself. I think I've realised that and there isn't many people that has. I'm a human being, I'm on this earth for my enjoyment. Nobody seems to think like that these days, very few of 'em anyway. You're supposed to be a right nice worker little vetch, as *The Clockwork Orange* said. You can just see it, pictures of t'typical average worker. The average person does this and the average person does that, you know. I find it a right laugh because when they talk about the average man in the street *I* aren't the average man in the street. Honestly it's something in me that tells me, I aren't the average man in the street. They might be on about somebody similar to me so it might apply to me, but I aren't the average man in the street. I'm somebody different.'

Maybe this culture is doomed in any case, ill-adapted as it is to a rational-bureaucratic world of anxious and orderly role-fillers, performers of minutely specified tasks and compliantly consuming consumers. Still, when I'm confronted with a manifestation like Barry's of its characteristic life and experience, I can't feel that it's my place to help push it down to its final demise. But here I'm aware that I part company with many teachers who, willing agents of 'mainstream society', need no encouragement to get in there and start imposing 'order' and 'seriousness' and 'sense of responsibility' on the whole anarchic, outmoded scene. Hence the running battles which typify schools' relationships with independent-minded working-class teenagers — despite the active critical intelligence which ought to mark many of them out as ideal subjects for education.

Still there have also always been teachers who have appreciated these students, some who, guided by their hearts and perhaps with an uneasy sense of betraying professional duty, have enjoyed their company, and some who, with their heads too, have found in them admirable and important qualities which school tends to undervalue or even to attack. It seems to me that any teacher who knows the students well and pays heed to his or her own human responses cannot do otherwise than respect their sense of their own autonomy and take that as the basis of the transaction. Who, once exposed in a moment of trust to the underlying seriousness and consistent style of a character like Barry, would *want* to cut through what is already happening in order to impose some preconceived scheme of learning? The informal education of these students is proceeding to their own satisfaction under their own direction. Given the right climate it will proceed in the classroom too, sometimes in its own habitual mode of social interaction with other members of the culture, sometimes drawing too on the modes of literate culture — reading and writing, the use of print and other media, the language of public communication.

In conceding to students who forcefully assert their own right to autonomy as much of it as is possible within the limits of compulsory attendance at school and at lessons, we do not have much to lose. The alternatives are the behaviour we are already so familiar with: active and passive resistance, and absenteeism. At worst these students will do nothing, which is what most of them effectively do now, in open or ingeniously disguised forms. At best, being intelligent and curious, they will take up possibilities we offer and achieve some educational benefit. At least we will remove the worst barbarities from the situation and make life more civilised for both sides.

'You were lucky, you, 'cause I didn't use to be as bad with you as what I was in t'other classes. I mean, with you I'd do nowt, but be behaved most of t' time, most probably just study about summat or read. In maths classes and that I were doing summat wrong all t'time. I wasn't doing my work. You know, stuffing paper down t'electric radiator and filling us out with smoke.'

But simply to abolish the most inhumane aspects of compulsion and leave the victims no less trapped in a situation which they see as a pointless waste of time is little gain. Autonomy becomes more than a mere formal absence of coercion when free agents who regard themselves as equals in respect of personal worth, if not of knowledge, feel themselves to be drawing new life from their relationship. Many of us who have not found it hard to accord respect to students whose qualities genuinely excite our admiration can testify to the enjoyment and learning we have derived from them. It is perhaps less easy but nevertheless important to be clear what they can gain from us.

Minimally, as I have already implied, we can be the ones who clear a space for them, who get school off their backs for a while. An interlude in which you are not told what to do at every turn and can be yourself may be an important relief. Next, we can reflect back, amplify and bestow legitimacy on their experience, concerns and strengths. As ones who are held to be insiders in the ambivalently-regarded world of 'proper' knowledge and educated culture, we are in a position by listening to our students and taking them seriously to convey to them that their accounts are no less substantial or real and have no less validity than those of the 'qualified' people whose words fill the books and media. They benefit from seeing us benefit from what they show us.

Our last contribution, obvious as it may appear, is knowledge. We have knowledge of the world of public knowledge and knowledge of the forms in which experience, thinking and learning may be expressed. This knowledge does nothing for them if it is presented remorselessly according to a programme, without regard to the separate immediate interests of individuals. But with a flexible and responsive teacher who at the right moments comes up with information, ideas, books and ways of doing things which answer directly to present needs, lively students can experience new knowledge as extension after extension of their own insights and powers. When we are able to do this for them — and how much good is all our arduously acquired learning if it cannot be brought to illuminate some normal adolescent curiosities and questionings? — we can take it that the relationship is on a healthy basis.

Often with these working-class 'freelances' the breakthrough into productive school work comes when they realise simultaneously that their own experience and culture can be a source of value and interest and that they are themselves capable of articulating that experience. The first significant production may be in talk or in writing. A typical pattern is shown by the case of Robert, a 15-year-old boy who found himself, as a member of a small group which included the teacher, after many sessions in which trust had built up slowly, talking uninterrupted for over four minutes about an incident he had been involved in one Saturday night. It was a *tour de force*, and was recognised as such by the group, who sat back and enjoyed the performance. Part of it went

> '. . . and when he got round t'pictures I goes, Right, I'm going to get him. We shot across t'car park and there's like this alleyway, you know, near t'Tesco, and we went up there and I'm looking round for him, waiting for him, and he hasn't come, and I thought, Oo, I wonder if he's gone back . . . and we sees Tyson walking along like, tha knows, and I got round t'side of t'thingy . . . and he's coming closer and closer, and I starts walking round, and he'd just come into view and I, splash! with t'sour milk all over him. He turns round and he goes, "You dirty git!" I chucks some more on him and some more and he looks round, he were like that, and he looks round and I chucks some more and it hit him in t'face and he comes flying at me as mad as an ox and he grabs me and milk's flowing all over t'place and t'milk bottle goes flying and smashed, and I were fighting with him and I pushed him and banged his head on t'side of t'thingy, up t'side of this wall, and er Firth goes, "Gi' up now! Gi' up now! Gi' up! Break it up!" and Tyson goes, "Look at me! Look at my coat! Sour milk doesn't come off owt!" '

As the tape recorder was left on as a matter of routine in these sessions, precisely in case something like this came up, the story was preserved and could be replayed and typed out. After previously producing only the most perfunctory written work, Robert now made himself

into a writer and wrote his autobiography, twenty-five sides of A4
paper in length. Perhaps the best section was about his sister's
wedding, which began . . .

'During 1973 I think the thing that stands out most was my sister's
wedding. It fell in October. My day started off by me having to go
with one of Clive's friends in Clive's car to pick up my grandad
Fisher from the old men's home at Sandal. Then when we brought
him to our house I had to wash and change and, the worst, I had to
wear a tie and a button hole. Is tha ready? asked Dave Clive's friend
who was driving his car. Aye, a spose so, I replied. He said, Right
lets go down to Clive's then. As I walked down the yard I remember
thinking, Aw God, I hope none o'me mates see me like this. If they
do I'll never live it down.

When we arrived at Clive's I was surprised. The house was in a mess
and there was Clive sitting on the sofa scruffy as a scare crow and
watching Laurel and Hardy.'

Paul used to talk about his village. He decisively got going as a writer
when he got (from me) the general idea of a form in which to display
his knowledge and feelings:

Contents

Section 1 — the view of the village from a high building, the things
that happen, the place Sharlston itself.

Section 2 — A couple from down south — their view of the village —
and what they think about it as they pass through in their car.

Section 3 — A miner walking home from a hard day's digging away
at coal. What he does, how he walks, the things that happen etc.

Section 4 — Slides: did some slides and did a tape recording about
them.

Section 5 — Map or plan of New Sharlston. Number different points.
Write about the different points.

The sort of thing he wrote as commentary to the slides was

2. In this slide there is no smoke coming out of the pit chimney but
usually there is. There's a cold misty fog overhead. When I was
young we had great games on them logs but I once cut my leg on
them.

6. This is a typical garden in New Sharlston. The vegetables are coming up fine in that rich black soil. A green-house rotting to bits besides a heap of manure.

7. You can't see anyone in the club at the back of the slide but I promise you there will be a lot of men and women boozing and getting drunk. I remember one night when I saw a drunken man walk straight across the road without looking and nearly got run over.

Paul went on to write in a similar way about Pontefract Races. Sections included

From arriving at the racecourse to going through the turnstiles.

Placing a bet — how to put a bet on etc.

On the way home in the car talking about the day's racing etc.

By now he saw himself as a writer to the extent of consciously 'collecting material' when he was out:

The bookmakers were now in the racecourse and setting up their stalls. I chose one particular one and described him. He had a pair of checked tartan trousers and a blue sweater and brown pointed shoes. He had a smiling face with a moustache and a bald head, he had a red tartan hat on his head but I knew he was bald because I had seen him at the races before. He had a big fat cigar in his mouth. So you could tell he was making money on the horses.

Some guidelines suggest themselves for conducting education with independent-minded working-class adolescents. The curriculum may have to be negotiated, not imposed, at least at the level of the topics within the subjects. The wider the field over which the student may exercise discretion, the easier it will be to get significant activity going; thus it can be helpful, for instance, if several subject courses are somehow grouped together and run as a single block. Conventional demarcation lines must not be allowed to get in the way of a student's explorations — those, for instance, between 'factual learning' and 'creative response'. We need to be prepared provisionally to sacrifice 'balance' and 'breadth' for the sake of uninterrupted concentration on the topics which seem most likely to give the student an experience of substantial genuine learning. And in our search for the topics that may release the motivation which we must believe to be latent in all students we may have to go outside the usual contents of the school curriculum.

So we must learn to live without the *course* — the arrangement whereby a teacher can present a planned sequence of knowledge and experiences over a long period to a captive audience; and without the *lesson*: no matter how lightly handled, enlivened with humour and so on, this is a basically teacher-directed form which organises students according to an imposed programme. It treats students all alike and cuts across independent lines of activity; it puts the teacher in an impersonal public role which is alien to the tastes and styles of many adolescents. The alternative mode is face-to-face conversation with individuals and small groups. The price of this renunciation is of course high: lessons have provided some students and teachers with exhilarating experiences. If we *can* use that form occasionally without producing resentment or glazed expressions, then we no doubt will; but I have seldom found that I could.

A relaxed and approachable teacher moving easily amongst a class who converse freely as they all work at the identical worksheet which the same teacher has produced is not the vision I have in mind. The change from the traditional pedagogy has to be one not only of style but of structure, whereby students actually become the autonomous agents working by choice which the informal teacher manner seems to credit them with being. Nevertheless, style counts, as Barry's statement makes clear, and it seems important to avoid in our behaviour those characteristics so readily associated by students with school as a mean-spirited, life-denying institution: the nagging, the checking up, the walking around with lists, the continuous poison gas cloud of petty interdictions, criticisms and controls.

But the traditional support which is hardest to live without is the 'work ethic', the moral imperative everywhere in the air in school which states that work is what one *ought* to do. We have to find other motivations for work simply because the appeal to the work ethic, having been made so many times — and too often quite transparently as a control ploy — no longer cuts any ice. Nor, as Barry makes clear, does the 'enlightened self-interest' version: 'work hard to get qualifications and get on in life.' For the alienated students we are considering, work needs to be there as a source of satisfaction and a means of fulfilling direct purposes, or not at all. We may have to learn that 'doing nothing' may be less destructive of a personal sense of purpose than 'work' done merely for the sake of appearances.

4 A new social reality

In September 1975 a team of us in the humanities 'faculty' (English, history, geography, religious education, social studies) at Shayhill High School put into operation a scheme which attempted to reflect the ideas outlined in the previous chapters. The school served four Yorkshire villages which contained established mining communities and new residential estates. When I arrived it was a secondary modern; then, two years later, it went comprehensive, starting with that year's eleven-year-old intake. The students we worked with on the course now to be described were from the pre-comprehensive 'creamed' population: they were the 150 fourteen-year-olds who formed the fourth year and who became the fifth year twelve months later.

The viewpoint I am presenting is my own, and my colleagues of the time may or may not wish to associate themselves with it. But the achievements I record were the work of a team of teachers — I pay tribute now to their efforts; and the whole venture was only made possible by the support of our headmaster and by the generous timetabling and staffing provided by the director of studies.

In this chapter I describe the organisational structure we devised and the new climate, new relationships and new ways of behaving which resulted. Chapter 5 will examine the educational outcomes in terms of the criteria I have been proposing: student choice, self-motivating activity, writing and talking to aid thinking and learning, student preoccupations as starting-points. Finally Chapter 6 will present two case-histories and venture some conclusions.

The mechanics of the scheme were as follows.

We got together a full-time team of six willing participants with a range of specialisms; regrettably they were all men. Each of us had a group. In addition, the head of history was timetabled to be with us for several periods to run the history course, and the senior mistress and youth tutor joined us part-time.

Our time was in quarter- and half-day blocks, amounting to almost a third of the timetable, and was labelled 'Humanities' — confusingly, since that was also the title of one of the CSEs that was included in the course. We made up mixed-ability groups of 25. Within them students worked largely on individually negotiated assignments directed towards '16+' English and CSE Humanities. They could also opt to withdraw from the group for part of the time to take conventional two-year courses in history and/or geography. Formally, the students' time was seen as disposable between three components, according to four alternative patterns:

English + history + geography

English + history + humanities

English + geography + humanities

English + humanities + more humanities

The whole thing depended on the availability of examination by course work assessment. We were able to participate in a '16+' scheme for English run jointly by our CSE board and the Joint Matriculation Board, under which certificates for both CSE (grades 1—5) and O Level (grades A—E) were awarded for course work. For history, geography and humanities we had Mode 3 CSEs. Humanities could earn one or more credits, entitled simply 'Humanities' or 'Humanities (social studies)', 'Humanities (environmental studies)' or 'Humanities (religious studies)'. The syllabus was relatively unspecific about content, allowing students to study almost anything, but with tightly defined criteria for assessment, in terms of skills, presentation, originality and so on.

We had six rooms, mainly close together. Almost the only inelegance in the arrangements was that Andrew, the head of geography, had to evict his own group at times in order to teach the geography group; we split them between the rest of us. What with withdrawals to history and geography, and others sometimes to the part-time team members for special projects, and some students working off the premises, it can be seen that the groups we were left with could sometimes be quite small.

Our main procedural principle was to allow the maximum amount of individual autonomy permissible within the system. There was at minimum an underlying feeling, and in some of us an explicitly articulated belief, that we should try to make all our transactions with students positive ones. Our efforts should be directed towards education — the promotion of skills, personal qualities and attitudes, awarenesses and knowledge — and not towards secondary institutional aims such as enforcing 'appropriate' behaviour: the justification for forcing people to come to school was not after all for them to be made to be quiet or to take their outdoor coats off or to have entries made about them in a teacher's book. Only the actual promotion of learning could be chalked up to our credit, yet our experience was that teachers generally put a surprisingly small part of their effort *directly* into that. So as against conventional wisdom which interprets occurrences of non-educational activity — e.g. social chat, doing nothing — as evils which need to be actively countered with teacher time and energy, we tried to regard them neutrally, as the simple non-occurrence of the sought-after activity: only if such behaviour was causing an obvious problem to others would we intervene. If nothing harmful was going on, that would be a satisfactory base to work from; if educational things happened, then we were climbing up into the pluses, with each additional manifestation an extra bonus. And for the students, each encounter with a teacher should also be a plus, an experience which if not useful would at least be pleasant or enlivening.

Four of the rooms were around a central landing; this area was felt to be the hub of things. The doors were generally open and there was a regular traffic of students passing between them with educational or social intentions. Music could be heard from Graham's room — latest rock LPs, taped in the small hours — and within one could sometimes glimpse a student lying reading on a mattress. The landing itself was a meeting place for those who wanted to be out of the teacher's eye, and was also sometimes taken over by groups of girls with chairs who wanted to read together. Reading was much in evidence as a favoured activity around the classrooms — and it was possible to read for two or three hours at a stretch and to get through whole books. Talk went on everywhere: on the landing, around tables, on the cupboards, in standing and seated clusters, as the sole activity of a group or accompanying work. Writing went on in most of those locations too. The teacher would generally be in amongst it, or sitting at his desk whilst students sat on it or around it, in chairs or on other desks they had pulled up. The furniture was rearranged each session by large numbers of ad hoc adjustments. The rooms were untidy, with students' overcoats, army packs and shopping bags around the place; tables were pushed together and moved apart without concern for neat patterns or apparent aesthetic discomfort at the odd chair left isolated in the middle of an empty space. The walls and flat surfaces were not rich with pinned-up work or exhibited objects, nor was the environment in any way suggestive of a progressive primary school. It was more like a mess-hall or students' union — scruffy, adaptable, multi-purpose and evidently comfortable to the users.

> I couldn't have worked in a nice little desk positioned in a nice little place.
> Better have your desk in t'middle of t'classroom.
> Take it where you wanted, I mean, if you enjoy working in one end of t'classroom work in one end of t'classroom, get yourself sprawled across a desk. If that's t'way you're going to produce better work, why not?

Folders covers, which might have meticulously respectable work inside, were elaborately customised on the outside with graffiti, initials, doodles, cartoons and pop stickers, as if mediating the private, reflective world of the contents and the working-class youth culture all around.

Some students would normally work, or not work, in large groups. Others stayed in pairs for the whole two years. Individuals would often shove a table to one side to be on their own for an hour or two. Only occasionally would the group of twenty-five be the working unit. Sometimes seventy or eighty would pile into one room for a film or TV programme, but it would be fairly rare to find a teacher addressing a complete seated and attentive group. If we read to them, some would still be moving around, leaving for better scenes in other rooms, rifling through our desk drawers for the keys to the cupboard where their personal reserved books were kept, or going to the window for a lungful of fresh air and a gaze at the vast restful spread of rural-industrial landscape.

Far more than in normal classrooms, laughter was a feature of the scene. Students laughed at their own, each other's and the teacher's expense, clowned, read out funny bits from books and their own stories, re-enacted experiences, and spun non-stop humorous commentaries on the life and work of the classroom. Occasionally the laughter, and sometimes a serious discussion or argument, would spread and take over the whole group, producing moments when a collective identity could be felt even though we and they habitually related individually and in small friendship clusters. Then the situation would fragment again, and small groups, pairs and individuals would resume talking, quietly thinking, reading, writing and drawing, having crises, dogging the teacher to get supplies or help — and laughing.

Two extracts from a log which I kept about my own group may help to convey the feel of these humanities lessons:

Friday 16th January

Graham & Andrew were out on a visit but it didn't seem to affect things. Good day.

Afternoon a bit ragged — me too knackered to do much. Read them a story period 6 ('Nice old-fashioned romance') and another to Tony Norris's group (Paul Kirkman, David Absolom) period 7 ('Butch minds the baby').

Darren had best day yet, writing about horse-races — Jim's doing. (Darren worked mainly with Jim.) Kept at it, calm, refused to work with Steven Ellis in afternoon. One of success criteria should be sustained calm pre-occupation, *chosen*, without pressure, in natural social situation. (Mel Young has been able to achieve this sometimes, drawing, especially when Roy's around.)

Don't know what the drugs lot did — not very much, I think.

Helped Christine and Julie on and off with deviance stuff. They seemed to be getting somewhere by tackling difficult material.

John Settle came. I'd said I'd try to have something new ready (to follow China) — about modern history, but I hadn't. He saw me and Jim — wants us to provide two lots of work. We agreed (John's own idea) on something anthropological — primitive cultures.

Joe Patchett has written a nice little piece about the general scene at Sharlston.

Quite a few on Community Service. Didn't make much contact with Mick, Mel, Barry & Co.

Still haven't talked to Diane. Carol getting interesting — commenting and initiating more.

Michael want to Sharlston Pit with camera in afternoon. Also Karen and co.

Hannah and Susan to island in Nostell Dam.

Paula and Pamela out looking at houses. Paula wrote in log that fed up because Pamela just wanted to skive.

two of the team

by William Saroyan

by Damon Runyon

Jim, one of the team

Roy, youth tutor and part-time member of the team

He was in Graham's group.

Janet still seems to be reading *Catcher in Rye*. And Carol. Seemed to be reading to Mel part of time.

by J.D. Salinger

Mick, Mel & co. did a bit of reading of *Beaverbird*.

Penguin Take Part Books

Wednesday 28th January

Mel wrote a true story about camping last week . . . in connection with countryside project. I'd marked it lightly. He wanted it fully corrected so he could copy it out, so I did, and he did, very quickly. Asked me to look after it but instead I gave him new folder.

Told Mick I wanted to type his out, so he had to tell me a couple of words I couldn't read. Chuffed. Not sure what he went on to do. Sam writing something (first for months) on countryside. Barry wrote a bit in log; suggested he might take photos of countryside, and write about a day out with dog and gun. Said what he's interested in is pollution of the countryside. Probably he'll be interested in all the FoE stuff — he must talk to Andrew.

Friends of the Earth, Andrew — teacher

Michael working off posters from NCB. Waiting for developer to do his film. Said I'd do it.

Helen was writing something (miner's day); Susan took sheet of English ideas, started on 'The Prisoners'. Yvonne had t'monk on.

was in a bad mood

Karen N. & her friend Tina Clough wanted new project. Took a time as they had no ideas, except they fancied going out. Roughed out something on ways of life in different places (different areas round Wakefield). They were to rough out plans.

Tina: from another group

Janet — talk at last. *Catcher in Rye* she's still reading and she says it's getting better. *Possibly* interested in taking CSEs seriously. Suggested wrote thoughts on book as she went along, as a log. Got her to try deviance stuff.

Mary and Tracy want to start something on Wakefield on Friday. I suggested a survey of a small area, e.g. down Westgate.

Darren has been doing a load of work at home (he says) assisted by 3rd year, Paul Bebbington, who does good drawings. Worked today on writing down something on horse-racing in Siena that Roy had told him. Suggested he take camera to Haydock Park on Saturday. Resolutely refuses to read Paul's project on Pontefract Races.

Alec wants new project, but I told him to write an assessment of the old one first. (Must show them some of that Countesthorpe self-assessment from the book.) Agreed on China. First move, Neil to teach him what he knows, and tape the proceedings, starting Friday. Neil dubiously agreed. Gave Alec Roberts to start on.

Paul Kirkman: has done best work yet on the 'deviance' sheet, and I asked him in log to write review of how he's getting on.

Joe Patchett announces he's on sharks. (Must give him MacCaig poem.)

Paula and Pamela went to see another Walton lady; but turns out her kids now go to school; so came back.

Christine and Julie — gave Julie next Deviance stuff: 'soccer hooliganism' sheet, asking for comments and imaginary interview. (Brian says he understands my notes on Taylor's articles on soccer hooliganism and doesn't agree. His views will come out in his fictitious interview with Ian Taylor, he says.)

See Chapter 3

Schools Council Project Writing across the Curriculum 11–16 *Keeping Options Open* Ward Lock 1976
Roberts E.M. *Mao Tse-tung and the Chinese Commu-nist revolution* Methuen
Norman MacCaig 'Basking Shark' — or perhaps it was 'Power Dive'

These entries were written when the project was well under way and give a taste of its notable features. With long stretches of time at our disposal (e.g. most of Friday) and groups of 25, we were in a position to think about the students individually rather than administer them in the mass. Very occasionally we would deal with the group as a whole (e.g. reading a story); more often with small groups (including reading to them); and perhaps most often with individuals. Students on the whole organised themselves, once their work had been set up; they did not come into the room and wait for us to get them started. We tried to stay off their backs and did not attempt to keep tabs on everything that was going on, sometimes losing effective contact with an individual for several days. The work which was in progress at any one time was very diverse, and so were the resources in play. Work identifiable as 'English' was mixed up with social studies and geography. Assignments originated from the students' own initiatives, from discussions with the teachers and from pre-prepared sheets and packs. We, the teachers, spent our time mainly in conversation, explaining and instructing, making suggestions, listening, chatting and joking. On the whole we coaxed students along, and rarely directed them. Students were allocated to a group, but did not have to stay in it all the time; they had access to other teachers and to friends in other groups, and some availed themselves of this option to organise congenial work and congenial company for themselves. It was quite easy for students to go out of school on assignments, as well as on organised expeditions in the minibus. It was also easy for them to 'waste time' if they were inclined to. Partly as a result, there was little disruptive behaviour. Time could also be 'wasted' in other ways, as when projects undertaken by students failed to work out, and when administration broke down in the face of the complexity of what was going on — developer run out, preschoolers earmarked for study discovered to have started school, work not ready.

Thus it was an imperfect world, containing a mixture of successes and failures, some of them of the old varieties, some strikingly new; but unarguably a world considerably removed from the settings in which most 14-to-16-year-olds find themselves.

It perhaps sounds an anti-intellectual climate. But amidst the social life one would have found that pointing out poems to each other in books, browsing through the filing cabinet and reading the extracts and stories, arguing over politics, reading a story together in turns and passing round each other's essays were as much typical components of the culture as were the joking and the gossiping — quite apart from the considerable amount of writing that went on. Certainly at times the mood could be one of apathy, sometimes of rowdiness, but more typically the climate suggested normal relaxed adolescent interaction, with the modes of behaviour that usually implies. In addition, it included serious educational activity without any sense of artificiality or strain.

The same measures which made it a good scene for adolescent life tended also to produce distinctive educational pay-offs. Students valued their freedom of movement. Some hardly ever availed themselves of it, some at first abused it (by disappearing to other parts of the school, forcing us into a policing role we hadn't wanted), but a great many used it in positive ways. It enabled John Settle (referred to in the log extract) to obtain the services of a number of teachers; it allowed people from other groups to listen to the stories read in my room and students from all over to attend Andrew's geography lessons when he was onto a good topic; Gavin from Jim's group was able to team up with Brian in my group to work on a wildlife project together, a combination which had a good effect on Gavin's work; and when I was in a bad mood, students could get away from me. (Although we assigned students to groups at the start, many voted with their feet; usually we formalised the de facto arrangements they made and put people on the books of the teacher they had gravitated to.) The following type of unplanned occurrence was made possible by this freedom and was important in promoting new developments in a number of students (my log, 7th July 1976):

Darren did a tiny bit of his education work-sheet. Then Richard Ibbotson came in from Ken's group looking for some more duplicated stories to read, having much appreciated 'The Pool', Billy bit from *Slaughterhouse 5* and 'Anecdotes of John Cage'. Gave him some more; Darren asked for some. Richard recommended 'The Pool'. Darren sat on his own and read that, thought it was good, then I gave him 'The Moray' — long and hard — and he liked that too.

an Orwell extract

an extract from the autobiography of Arturo Barea

Richard kept coming, and graduated to books. Not normally one for school work, he used to take poems home that he liked and apparently passed them round his mates on the estate where he lived (a volunteer agent of cultural diffusion!). Many of the students that I worked most fruitfully with were not from my own group, and several of my own students did their best work for one of the other teachers.

Getting to know the other teachers was seen quite consciously by some students as part of the point. They would hear from friends about a particular teacher and say 'I must get to know this bloke' or 'I'd like to see this', and they would come along and present themselves, or their mates in your own group would bring them in and say 'This is Sue — she wants to see what it's like in here.' Similarly, we would sometimes visit another room and spend half an hour talking to the students there. This freedom was one of the most important features of the scene.

Intially, all our efforts went into getting students to talk and to reveal something of themselves, so that we could begin to propose possibilities and put before them material likely to appeal. Things would generally start with the teacher sitting down at the student's table. Often it would only be after a long talk or perhaps several sessions that we'd be able to say, 'OK, so this is what it's going to be.'

Sometimes we would take a short extract or a few poems to a small group and read them to them. Or we might simply leave them some material and say 'Have a look at this — I'll come back and see what you think.' We might mention the activities that could be involved in work on a topic: 'You could have a look at the nearest service station on the M1 — you could get there and back in a morning;' and in the course of such discussions a quite different possibility might occur to the student: 'My mate's a lorry driver and I've been with him — can I do something on that?' Or we might have to say, 'Go and look at what some of the others are doing,' or send them to see if any of the other teachers had any better ideas, or if students in other groups had any ideas.

Once a topic was agreed on, we would usually sit down with the student with a piece of paper and suggest ways of going about it, listing those that met with approval and those the student came up with. 'Use the indexes to find what there is about so-and-so . . . read such and such chapter . . . make notes . . . write a letter to Gandhi from the local British official appealing to him not to go ahead . . .' 'Stop at every fourth lamppost and record a quick impression of your surroundings, working from the centre of town to the first bit of farmland . . .' These bits of paper could be works of art; they were the vehicle for some of our most creative thinking, and in so far as preparation was possible for this sort of teaching it largely consisted of thinking up such strategies whereby students would be able to get a purchase on an amorphous topic. Initially, topics were often defined only in the most general terms. Helping the students to get into them involved coming up with particular ways of cutting through them. In order to avoid the mindless collection of useless data, it was necessary to make very specific searches or transects or samplings. 'Cars' had to come down to particular questions like (scribbled on the student's bit of paper): 'Range Rover and Rover saloon — what are the different values or self-images they're designed to appeal to? (Remind me to show you — bit about Citroen DS19 by R Barthes.)' A student who chose the musician Alex Harvey as a topic began by devising Alex's likely answers to interview questions I wrote down for him. ('Why are you so interested in dreams, Alex?' 'You're 40 — how do you explain the way the kids still go for you?')

As time went on we got better at these negotiations and went into them with more resources in the form of ideas that worked, materials we could lay our hands on and examples of work done by other students.

After the early stages, we did a surprising amount of the sort of thing that is conventionally thought of as teaching, except that we did it with individuals: i.e. we would sit down and tell people about things. For instance, we were able to pass on interesting bits of sociology that would have been inaccessible to our students in their original form. When Barry wrote in his log

Also been reading some Open University story with him [me] — about cab drivers and tipping

he means I *told* him about that sociological article in an OU reader while the book lay open in front of us.

Some of the educational transactions that typically passed between teachers and students are illustrated by more comments extracted from my own log:

Most interesting thing today was that in conversation with Sam and Mick, and Mel and Barry, it emerged that something on people's use of the countryside (i.e. them) would be a good project. Reading Brian Lawrence's and Stuart Thomas's pieces helped things along — they liked them very much. Also important: Sam declared that this round here wasn't country, but he was very attached to round Appleby, where he went to a farm (relations?) camping with his uncle. Great to go walking on your own. Obviously here is the sort of deep motivating preoccupation I've been waiting for. Wonder whether realistically there could be a career prospect? Said that was where *he* would be off when he was older — if he got a job.

Writing by former students

David Absolom gave him some advice about

difference between notes and discursive writing for his drugs stuff.

Alec Parrish had written a letter from the Red Indian chief. It was bitty and unshaped. I was able to show him so, making a list of the points he made and showing there was no sense in the order he introduced them in. I'd never done that before with him.

Barry had been (last Friday) to talk to Chris James. I saw his writing today which was good on how he entered the place and his first impressions of Chris, then thin on what he learnt from Chris. When we got talking, I explained a bit about people being partly the result of big social forces operating and so on, and the key thing about Chris that came out when Barry got talking was that Chris stood out as being completely indifferent to consumer values. Barry was really good, very serious and articulate. Couldn't he learn a lot about society by thinking deeply about a few individual biographies? . . . His account, duplicated, could be raw material for others.

Warden of a field studies centre but selected for interview simply as an interesting talker

There was more variety in our working relations with students than was normal in conventional classrooms. Of those who worked, some clearly did so as a concrete way of realising their interests, others out of a sense of virtue or academic ambition. Of those who did not work, some were on good terms with us and some were indifferent. (Few were hostile.) Of those who were indifferent to us, some worked and some did not. Still, a number of patterns emerged which can be described.

There was one group of lively and interesting students with whom we were constantly engaging in discussion and argument, who were eager audiences for our ideas and for the bits and pieces we brought in, who were active participants in 'the scene', who read books and who brought serious concerns into the classroom — but who could rarely be persuaded to write. (Most of them finally took up their pens at the eleventh hour, displaying in the last few weeks a fluency and competence which had developed in the near total absence of exercise, and producing enough work to earn themselves good grades in the assessment.) One such was Wayne in Graham's group. As Graham commented,

You could say he never did anything for one and a half years. He used to just read. Anything that I gave him he read. And he used to plan my lessons for me, say for the third years, in terms of poetry, things like that . . . . Then he suddenly thought, well it's about time I got some O Levels, or got some of my CSEs.

We learnt that putting pressure on such students to work was generally counterproductive. Left to themselves they derived benefit in their own way from the whole learning environment, and in the end they usually got their grades in any case.

Another group were more actively alienated from school: they rejected written work not because they found talking or reading intellectually more exciting but because it was a school institution which had no place in their conception of themselves. We nevertheless induced most of them to do some worthwhile things; then we lost them again in their last year.

But most students were workers, in varying degrees. Amongst them, what made the difference was whether strong interests were engaged; this was what largely determined what dealings between them and their teachers were like. With students whose real concerns were not brought into play, although they were often cooperative enough, affairs would typically proceed as they did with Alec. There was no doubt that Alec genuinely cared about cars, the topic he chose. He made a reasonable job of the numerous pieces of work he undertook, including lists of technical data, notes on *Working for Ford* by Huw Beynon, arguments for and against the private car, accounts of drag racing and car auctions, a criticism of British cars and a story about the effect of a fast car on a normally sober young man; but nearly every piece was separately suggested by me, and the project developed no momentum of its own. Alec's interest in cars never found satisfying expression in this work: it was simply no substitute for those evenings under old cars in his mate's driveway.

There were students who one would class as 'well-motivated' whose commitment was perhaps less to understanding the world than to the idea of 'acquiring education'. It was an image of themselves as diligent (and successful) students that seemed to inspire them rather than interest in the particular content, though that might develop. Such students tended to come back frequently for fresh instructions, and to accept suggestions with little question and work at them happily. It was not easy to get them to ask questions or puzzle about things, or to make their inquiries into personal enterprises. Our worksheet-based programmed packages (the family, war, education, deviance, China etc.), devised for other courses, worked well with these students; they liked them and learnt from them by treating them seriously as aids to learning rather than as tasks to be got through.

Julie's case will illustrate how we operated with hard-working students of this type. I usually found it necessary to be quite specific in suggesting what she might do. We never really got away from a relationship in which I 'gave her work'; we did not reach the point at which it was enough for the student to indicate an area and the teacher to throw out ideas, angles, considerations and approaches, after which the student would take it away and so something with it in her own way. Nevertheless it was a good educational relationship. Because Julie was so open to help I felt I was able to influence the way she wrote, studied and thought; I was invited to be in on the process at every stage in a way I was not with many others.

Maintaining contact with Julie was easy, even though she was often out at geography and technical college; she would seek me out in her free periods, and we also communicated successfully in writing. For instance, a tactic which would not have elicited much response from most students but worked well with Julie was for me to ask her questions, in writing. At one point I wrote

Very interesting. Can you write here
(1) *why we, in Britain, should bother our heads about primitive peoples. Would it matter if they died out?*
(2) *explain at more length the point you were making about the primitives having "no real jobs".*

This resulted in a worthwhile piece of clarification from Julie (the comments in italics are the ones I wrote in when I read the entry):

'I think that we in Britain should bother about primitive people, it would matter a great deal if they all died out. The reason for that answer is because primitive people know how to cure their own illnesses, which we ourselves are trying to discover. Special plants live in the jungle [*they don't all live in the jungle. Eskimos? Bushmen?*] and by mixing plant's leaves together they know how to make medicine. Because we need drugs, in the jungle is where the drug plants grow, and the primitive people know how to mix these drugs so it will keep their tribe healthy. So it does matter to us if the primitives die out.

What I meant by "no real job" was that they don't have to go to work at a certain time and they never have any holidays. Many people nowadays work five days a week, but primitive people work every day in order to live. If they go hunting and they do not succeed in catching anything, and they badly need food, they will not starve because plants which grow in the jungle provide them with food. In a way primitive people are civilised because if one person catches some food they will all share it, but, if that happened between us more than likely the person who got the food would keep it to himself.'

This reply revealed specific limitations of understanding which it was then possible for me to do something about. The last sentence offers an evaluation of her own which is not explicitly linked to my two questions, though it perhaps relates to the first: such volunteered comments, far from being regrettable irrelevances, are like gold in projects like this in that they represent the beginnings of a search for significance in the knowledge.

These entries from Julie's humanities log illustrate the general character of our relationship:

3/11/76 Wednesday

Would you give me some English please. Would you give me an interesting book to read, for example a humorous one. I have finished all my Geography off. We have done a great amount of work in Geography since September.

This morning I did some notes and a piece of English.

Can you give me some work on my project because I am getting bored with just taking notes and putting my own views down on paper. I would like to do something different with this project.

After Christmas I want to start a new project.

You now have "The Cowards". Do you still want a humorous book as well?
English – was what I suggested OK?
Project – OK – I'll work something out.

9/11/76 Tuesday

Yes, I still want a humorous book as well. Been doing Geography all afternoon.

Try "Billy Liar". I'll lend you it.

10/11/76 Wednesday

Today I started to answer those questions you set me on primitives but I am stuck so I will carry on with them on Monday with your help. [*Right*] So now I can do that other English you set me from the book "The Cowards".

See you on Monday morning.

Yep

The easiest students of all to deal with were the small group of those who were strongly motivated by interests and who found 'work' the natural way of fulfilling those interests. One felt they were engaged in a serious general enterprise of making sense of the world, and that any information which contributed to that enterprise was gladly received. It was not a question with them of seeking out *the* topic which would motivate the learning process, since all sorts of topics fed their general hunger for knowledge.

John Settle was an outstanding example of this type. His transactions with us were consultations, out of which he made up his own mind about what to do. Towards the end of the course he initiated studies of his own, not all of which we knew about until they were completed. He exploited the strengths of the system, shopping round three tutors as well as his own and getting them to set up projects with him. His file contains sections headed Housing and its problems, Teenager survey, Deviance, The weather '76, Crowded and uncrowded areas of the world, Pollution, Tanzania, China, Primitive cultures, A survey of housing in and around Wakefield and The world of wildlife.

Relations were different again with students who knew what they wanted to do and simply got on with it without letting us in. With some of these it was difficult to have any influence on what went on. Often enough plenty *was* going on, but sometimes it was within a rather narrow field: a succession of projects, for instance, with an exclusively local bias and entirely based on observation without any use of books. Attempts to get these students onto wider issues, or to show them how their topics were located in more general social or historical dimensions, often failed. The question repeatedly arose with us, wouldn't we be justified in insisting these students move outside parochial concerns? Our view was on balance that the price we would pay would be to lose the small residual fund of goodwill which was all we sometimes had to go on.

Finally there remained those who because of the opportunities afforded by our unusual set-up, after being perfunctorily involved or not at all, suddenly found an issue to set them alight and took their education into their own hands. Of this group more later.

5 Language and the forms of learning

Now I want to describe the students' work — or rather their educationally fruitful activity, since not all of this was seen as work. I take the central issues to be: What did the students actually do, since they were not doing many of the things which most students do most of the time? and, What difference did it make that English, with its emphasis on personal, expressive and imaginative uses of language, was intended to be realised across the whole humanities curriculum? I shall have most to say about two written modes of work, log books and projects, which developed in new ways and performed new functions; but first there are some points to be made about two other staple activities, reading and talking.

Our reliance on what I have called 'conversation' as the alternative to addressing whole classes may suggest that possibilities for teaching, and particularly for presenting literature, must have been seriously restricted. The conventions of what one can do face-to-face may seem to confine one to a low-key style of explanation, comment and dialogue and to deny one the advantages of the dramatic reading or the carefully structured introduction of information or material. In fact, conversation expanded to carry the educational functions that were required of it. It became a richer form, so that we could, for instance, without embarrassment sit down with individuals and read to them. In this way we could give poor readers a private experience of literature, and in general were able quite adequately to introduce books to students with the aim of encouraging them to read further. One of the advantages of our arrangements was that those who did were able to get on with it there and then, and sometimes to finish the book in a single session — a possibility inconceivable under our previous five-period allocation of English.

This morning I read a book on '19 is too young to die'. This book was very good and realistic. This book was about a girl of 19 and she had a blood disease called 'leukemia'. It was a long letter about her life while she had this disease. It was very good and I read it in 2 hours. (Student's log)

Occasionally we did read to the whole group, more often to smaller groups — a particular cluster of students who worked together or 'anyone who wants to come round and hear this'. Sometimes we would begin to read to a group in one part of the room only to discover after a few minutes that almost everyone was listening. An interesting example of the way appropriate social arrangements made themselves was what happened when I was reading episodes from Claude Brown's *Manchild in the promised land*, initially to half a dozen students but before long to most of my group. Those who did not want to hear it formed the habit of taking their work into another room, while members of other groups who had heard about it would come along for the occasion — sometimes sending a representative beforehand to find out what time I was planning to start.

Readings to a large audience were the closest we got to the traditional class treatment of a text. Discussion of literature and poetry certainly went on in small groups, but was not often of the type associated with literary analysis in the English literature lesson. A great deal of reading went on about which no formal work was done, though there were also some written studies of aspects of books. Our emphasis was on promoting wide experience of literature, and indeed on promoting reading of any kind as a chosen activity.

Poetry was a real presence in the classrooms, circulating informally, providing starting-points for writing and objects for written studies, and being much read aloud in small groups, by students and by teachers. I remember a Friday afternoon when for some reason the group was very small and we spent an hour or so doing nothing but reading poems to each other, sitting and standing casually around the room and every so often raiding the bookshelves and filing cabinet for more. It felt like the right way for poetry to be there.

Information books were important resources: their use will be referred to in the section on projects.

The space left by the withdrawal of the teacher from the best time-stretches, and all the interstices of private work, were filled by talk. It proceeded unrestrained. The teachers were part of it: we consciously tried to see that our talk was a real contribution to dialogue, and not simply teacher questions and admin comments. Students do not normally get the chance to talk to their teachers at length and on their own terms; ours did, and it meant a great deal to some of them.

It is hard to evaluate the effects of unrestricted opportunities to talk: it goes without saying that a large proportion of it had nothing to do with the ostensible task in hand. Much of the talk, I noted at the time, was

not educational in the sense of taking them out of their given world, extending their understanding of things outside that world, liberating them, if you like.
But it wouldn't need to be a very different sort of talk to do that, for them to make *educational* headway. Already some of their talk is serious, courteous and cooperative. It is these things because what is being talked about (problems and so on that touch them deeply) is something they care about. If wider matters were to come to be regarded in the same way, the discussion would be adequate to them without anything special having to be done about it.

And not infrequently that happened. The point was that

what is 'educational', and what is naturally occurring and spontaneous and flourishing because of its deep roots in the kids' lives and cultures, should be continuous, a seamless garment. It should be the same kid, equally being himself, who talks naturally about social class or transport policy and about what happened last night.

Ex-students, looking back on the course, claimed that they found themselves with more to say and more confidence to say it than their contemporaries, at work or in further education, who had been to other schools:

> You seem better socialised if you went to Shayhill School. Some people from the other schools have got basic characters, but they're not as, I don't know how to say it, worldly-wise — can I say that word?

> They're typecast. They've been to different schools, but they've same way of thinking, same outlook on life.

> They all seem like they've just been to school.

> They haven't had the chance to give their own opinions on things. They're just ready to accept.

Amongst the most interesting manifestations of the changed relationships and curriculum were unfamiliar forms of writing. I have mentioned how a conscientious student like Julie could keep in touch about her work through her log book, which seemed for her to perform two functions: administrative (keeping the supply of work flowing from me, checking that she's doing things in the right order, arranging consultations with me) and 'personal-confirmatory', for contemplating her own mounting achievements with satisfaction: 'Here I am, doing projects, being a student, coping with all this new work — it feels good.' Here is a sequence of entries relating mainly to Julie's project on 'Deviance', which was largely based on worksheets which I was producing at the time for use on a more formal social studies course:

6/1/76 Monday
Today I am starting a new project on associology which is about people and their way of life and many other things. I think this will be very interesting and I will hope to learn a lot. I will work very hard on this project but I will also carry on with my English work. I am glad you explained to me about this project because it has made my mind much clearer about it.

Yes, I think it will be a good one.
The word is "sociology" — to do with society, social life – man living together.

9/1/76 Friday
Today I started to work on the sheet called "The Cannabis Taboo". I have just started on the questions.
   I will be carrying on with this worksheet on Monday.

12/1/76 Monday
Today I had to write my own report. I did not put a Grade on because I do not really know what grade I should get.
   I also finished the worksheet on 'The Cannabis Taboo'.

and we had quite a long discussion about it. I like the way you've tackled this new work so far.

14/1/76
I have handed some English work in for you to mark. I will have a look at those sheets which you gave us.

15/1/76 Friday
Today I finished all the questions on the "DEVIANCE" worksheet. It was quite a good sheet, it took me 4 lessons to do it in. I like worksheets that you have to do plenty of writing for. This weekend I am going to write a piece of English.

I'm glad you liked the worksheet. I intend to do quite a few more.
But do you think you learnt anything from it? Could you write here what you got out of doing it?

Yes I have learnt something from these worksheets. I didn't know heroin was a serious drug but after reading these sheets I know now.

19/1/76 Monday
I think you have written a good report, I think it is very fair.
This morning I wrote some English.

23/1/76 Friday
Today I read those sheets on Drugs and information. I have found these very useful and I have learnt now some more information on Drugs.

26/1/76 Monday
Today I finished off some writing on a policeman and I having a conversation about drugs.

Excellent. I can't keep up with you.
The way I think the project will go is like this: we'll study a few examples of different groups of deviants. Drug-takers is the first, but we'll do others. Then I'll probably present you with some problem (some sort of deviant behaviour) and ask you to explain it.

28/1/76 Wednesday
Yes I think it will be a good idea how to go on with my project. I will be answering those 2 written questions you gave us tonight for homework.

Great. You're doing very well on this one.

30/1/76 Friday
I enjoyed reading the sheet on 'soccer hooliganism'.

4/2/76 Wednesday
I hope you have got some more worksheets for us, I find these sheets very interesting.

I'm finding it very hard going knocking these out fast enough to keep up with you. However, I'm trying — working on delinquency at the moment.

6/2/76 Friday
Today there were no Geography lessons so I stayed in humanities so I carried on with those questions which you gave us on Wednesday. Thank you for explaining the questions to us.
Anyway I have now finished those questions so I have handed it in to be marked.

9/2/76 Monday
I am really getting to like this project, I really like those typed sheets
you give us. I have really learnt a lot since I have been doing these
sheets, they are great.
I am pleased I decided to do this project.

*Yes, I get the impression you've learnt a lot too. So have I, reading the stuff in
order to write the sheets, and then having to explain them. I find sociology an
exciting subject to read at the moment.*
The next sheets are now ready!

18/2/76 Wednesday
Today I have been doing Geography all morning.
So I will see you on Friday so you can explain the second work sheet
on Juvenile Delinquency.

20/2/76 Friday
This morning I started to answer the questions on the Juvenile
Delinquency — second sheet but I would like you to explain this to
me. (Later) Now you have explained it to me I can understand the
sheet. Thank you. I am taking the sheet home to finish off because I
want to do that longer assignment at home so I can spend more time
on it and I can think about it more.

Another quite common type of log served no administrative function
and provided no record of accumulating work. It might best be
described as 'rabbiting on': a sort of written equivalent of gossip,
serving partly as a means of reliving events and partly as a way of
realising a relationship with the reader. From Susan's log:

10.3.1976
Thought I'd let you know that me and Paul are on speaking terms
again. Went for the dreaded jab. *God* was I scared. I could feel my
heart beating so fast. When I got in the room the nurse asked my
name and form. After that I was talking to Youngy. Before I knew it
it was all over — didn't even feel a thing. Then when she put that
rotten stuff in my mouth I nearly died-it was really rotten. Anyway
it's all over now. I wouldn't mind that kind of a jab again.

12.3.1976
This morning I went to the students and we had another one of
those meetings. Its really good fun going out to the students.
Probably if you took us on an interesting trip I would write about
what it was like and so add more work to my poor thin folder.
Crafty eh, what do you think, Pete?

Perhaps what Susan mainly used this channel to communicate was simply that it was *her* channel: she appropriated it in the same spirit that most students 'colonised' ambiguous spaces (theirs or the school's?) such as folder covers.

Some students used their logs as part of the way they worked on their topics, for raising questions and registering points. An example (Neil's) is reported in the next chapter. What *all* the habitual log-writers had in common was an enjoyment of that mode of communication. Neil put it:

> Oh great, I liked that because then you've got a direct relationship to the teacher, you can express what you like, better with writing than you can with words. You see, you've more time to think about it. I used to enjoy getting replies and writing new ones out.

It was not part of our original intention that students should work from worksheets and duplicated programmed courses, but as we had some to hand, and were still producing them for use on other courses in the school, inevitably they got used, quite heavily. Without them, the simultaneous demands of all the individually negotiated projects would probably have been too much. We half-distrusted them because we knew they could lead to a rather mechanical task-completing approach and preempt the students' own ways of making sense of a topic. However, in this scheme they were not used in the usual compulsory way but were simply made available as options: thus those who took them up tended to be ones who had some commitment to learning about the topic and generally avoided mindless blank-filling. In fact, some of these 'units' were quite successful, and tasks set in them elicited some of the most thoughtful and imaginative writing which was produced.

Nevertheless, students working on their own essentially meant to us *projects* — explorations in which the structuring was performed from scratch by each student, or by student and teacher together, and in which the source-material did not come ready organised for the particular purposes of the learner. In this form of work lay many dangers: in our past experience projects had meant laboriously written-out versions of information from books; and other pitfalls became apparent as we worked. We had to learn for ourselves how to help students organise projects so that they would result in learning and not mere production, and modify some of our preconceptions about the sort of concerns that are appropriately developed through that form at the age of 14–16.

We tried to make it a clear objective that projects should be a

means of understanding and not simply of 'getting a project done'.
To be justified, the written side of the project had to add something
worthwhile to the learning which could be achieved simply by
reading or observation or talking to people. Certainly, assessment
dictated that there had to be some sort of concrete deposit left behind
by the process, but the writing should nevertheless be primarily an
aid to learning rather than to marking. In particular, the recording of
information should be kept in its place: most projects we had seen
consisted of nothing else. Its functions should be to help the student to
distinguish what was important/ in the material, and to build a
resource to be drawn on for subsequent purposes — and that meant
for real use in the course of the project, and not for some vague
potential use at an undetermined future date. In general there
seemed to be three ways in which writing could help: first in note-
taking; and here the essential point was that a schematic,
abbreviated, quickly done form, which could display graphically the
relationship between the points, was far more useful than continuous
prose; and secondly in the noting of questions, puzzles, reflections,
comments and memos — 'interrogating the text' and performing a
running commentary alongside it, in writing; finally, there needed to
be an opportunity for something to be made of all the information
after it had been gathered: it needed to be applied to the elucidation
of some problem, or at least its implications and significance needed
to be explored and a personal evaluation of it made. Gradually, we
learnt to explain to students the alternatives to copying and
paraphrasing the books. Various approaches emerged, but common
to them was the insistence that *the information* was not the key part of
the project, but rather what the student did with it.

One format which proved workable was the three-part project.
Section 1 was reflections, questions, comments etc. about the work,
and a record of its progress: the appropriate form was a log, addressed
to the teacher (teacher as resource and support, not teacher as
assessor). Section 2 was the information, written in a note form
designed for quick recording and easy consultation, and not for
continuous reading by someone else. Section 3 was finished and
considered writing intended for a wider audience, containing
conclusions, interpretations and applications. Essays might be
appropriate here, but so might fictional and imaginative forms.

I can best exemplify how these ideas worked out by indicating how
a number of actual projects were made up.

Julie's project on primitive peoples followed this pattern. Its
contents were:

Section 1   Introduction of the "Challenge of the Primitives"
            written by Robin Clarke and Geoffrey Hindley. What I
            have learnt from the Introduction.
            Project log.
            Answers to questions (teacher's)

Section 2   Notes on *Primitive Societies* by F. Quilici
            Challenge of the Primitives
            Guardian article, "Threatened tribe opts for death"
            Survival International magazine

Section 3   Essay: "Primitives"

Brian's project on world wildlife in danger was similar, except that in
Section 3 he had an invented script for a television programme,
which included the commentary from a piece of documentary film
and a debate between a conservationist and a hunter.

John Settle did not have a Section 3 (public writing) for each
project. Instead, he grouped together at the end of his folder a
collection of essays on most of his projects, with a contents list and
explanation:

A List of ESSAYS from Projects

1. Demand for land.
2. Convenience foods.
3. Is it the house you want?
4. Living in poverty.
5. 'Subsistence' living.
6. Living from our needs.
   (The way I'd like to live) FREE
7. My views on DEVIANCE
8. The Best of British [about British weather]

An essay within a project is basically a summary of the work I have
done. Essays also contain my personal views on a particular subject.
I.e. convenience foods, these may be foods which cost twice as much
to be convenient, perhaps, than they would've cost as a simple food.
Personally I think a project is uncomplete without an essay, or a
sum-up of ideas, something which not only contains the facts, but
also my views on the subject.
Some of the essays which are listed are not necessarily follow-ups to
projects, some are based upon simple ideas which I found
interesting.

It was one of the main strengths of the project as a form of work that it could evolve in response to the changes in the student's awareness which the work itself was bringing about. Students sometimes discovered interests as they went along which they could not have named when they started and had possibly never before given a thought to; this form of work allowed them to pursue the new direction (and to record their reasons for doing so).

It was at those points, when students left the course they had originally prescribed for themselves or had been following at a teacher's suggestion and opted to investigate an issue they had themselves pinpointed, that we were conscious of autonomy as a positive achievement, a state won by the student out of his own development. Such a point was when John, after an extended period of reading and note-taking about housing in the Third World, decided to write this essay applying what he had learnt to his own environment.

Is it the house you want?
After past experience of noisy discontented neighbours a simple social problem or question springs into mind; 'Is it the house you want?' This I have wanted to put forward to so many neighbours in the past.

There is always something which needs doing, or some great improvement which is under way. For example one Sunday afternoon I took a slow observant walk around the estate on which I live. I couldn't help noticing just how many people were at work with an odd job in the way of improvement. I also noticed exactly how many homes had extensions, alterations and other fancy extras.

This all goes to show that people are never satisfied with their homes, and perhaps never could be. Among the most common extras I noticed was a simple divider of a living room and a dining area. All the other alterations or extensions ranged from this simple divider to loft conversions. It finally occurred to me that people were willing, and indeed paid hundreds of pounds, to alter the basic site of their home.

From this we can see that a house is not a home until the occupants have had a say in its appearance. Perhaps it would be better to provide small plots of land on which people could not only build, but plan their own homes. At least these would not need altering, or extending; or would they? If this idea was sent off to Parliament I wonder what the reply would be.

Personally I think if there is the slightest chance an occupant could build his own home on his own land, the chance is worth fighting for. Perhaps the occupants of such a building would still not be satisfied. It is a big probability that alterations would still be made.

As I observed the different dwellings I asked myself, Why do people alter their houses? I found this was very difficult to answer and thought of the many possible answers. Perhaps the extended area was too small previously? Maybe the residents wanted a change of appearance? Or possibly just to beat the neighbour?

It was difficult to decide but I think probably above all, an extension is made as a change, to make a house more exciting.

If people were able to build their own homes I think the probability of an alteration would still be left very high. I would, however, still prefer to build, and plan my own home, and grow my own vegetables, maybe live off my own back, unlike a parasite.

There are too many parasitic people who are supported by others; I think this could prove to be a dangerous situation.

But it was Brian who provided the classic example of the evolution of a project, an evolution corresponding to the emergence of new awarenesses and confidence.

On September 3rd 1975 (i.e. at the very start of the course) Brian began a project on football clubs which meant making charts of data about all the clubs from Aldershot to York City. In fact he did it twice: he transferred the information from his source book into a rough book at home, then onto paper in school. Needless to say, it took some nerve on my part to refrain from intervening. This activity was still recorded (in his log) as continuing on December 15th, but that is the last mention until on February 4th he states: 'Today I decided that the work I started earlier in the year on all the football clubs in the league was not worth finishing.' From the beginning, however, other football-related bits of work had been done from time to time; at first, these were seen as very much sidelines to the main project, but what happened was that they grew in importance, moved out of an expressive and into an inquiry mode and took over the project. The stages in the development can be seen from this chronology, which I have compiled with the help of Brian's log:

10 Sept	Wrote about "my first football match".
8 Oct	Made up a football crossword.
22 Oct	Wrote a story about a match which included an

10 Nov   account of hooliganism by supporters.

10 Nov   Started a story "The Supermatch"

14 Nov   In my folder I found a note from Mr Medway with various suggestions that I thought were good ideas and I'm going to start working on them as soon as I have finished the story "Supermatch".

19 Nov   I have started an interview which is about hooligans and there is a part where the hooligan is interviewed like you suggested. (This was a fictional television interview.)

28 Nov   Interviewed his grandfather who had supported Huddersfield Town all his life. Transcribed the interview, which ran to many pages.

7 Jan   Wrote a piece about "What I think they have to do" to get "Match of the Day" together.

19 Jan   I read about Hooliganism by Ian R. Taylor. He says what he thinks about hooliganism and I agree with some points so I am going to do some work on that.

Ian Taylor is a sociologist, and the article I showed Brian suggests that the 'hooligans' are in fact the 'rump' of the traditional working class supporters who at one time identified solidly with the local teams but have now largely drifted away: only the 'hooligan' has retained the passionate loyalty which was once general. This view of the hooligans as custodians of the tradition is supported by Taylor's claim that they know more about their clubs' history than do the average supporters.

26 Jan   Today I started my work on hooliganism. I am going to do the story as a television talk-in show with an old dedicated football supporter and Ian R. Taylor.

He wrote a transcript of the programme. It begins:

Interviewer   Tonight on *Talk-in* we have a 75-year-old member of the public who has supported Stoke City since he was 7 years old. Welcome to *Talk-in*, Mr Smith

Mr Smith   Thank you, it's good to get a chance to say what I feel.

Interviewer   And our guest tonight is sociologist, Ian R. Taylor. Thanks for coming, Ian.

Ian R. Taylor   Good to be back.

Taylor makes the point about the resentment felt by supporters that their game has been taken from them, and about the *recent* amplification by the media of a violence that was always there; Mr Smith (whose views to some extent reflect those of Brian's grandfather) asserts that the violence really has increased and that the answer is stiffer penalties.

This format was entirely Brian's idea. The log entry above was the first I heard of it. I wrote back that it was a great idea, and also: *I'm not absolutely convinced by Ian Taylor's ideas, but I think you could work out a survey about 'hooligans' which might reveal more of the truth.*

4 Feb   Today I decided that the work I started earlier in the year on all the football clubs in the league was not worth finishing, but instead I am going to do a set list of questions for every club in the football league. I will answer the questions by asking people, from books and from what I know myself. When I have done this for every club in the football league I will go back to my work on hooliganism and I will ask people (who are likely to fight at football matches) questions on the club they support. I will also ask other people who are just quiet and wouldn't give anybody trouble, the same questions and see who knows the most. This will prove who are the supporters that know most about the club's history.

He went ahead with preparing the questions.

  8 March   I have decided to make all my football project into a kind of book, with the first section on trying to prove Ian R. Taylor's views wrong.
12 March   As a result of a suggestion of mine, he wrote a piece on "Hooliganism as I see it".
15 March   Wrote "what my aim is":

'. . . So Ian R. Taylor thinks that these are the real supporters and know most about the history of their club. I totally disagree with that and think that the quiet fans know most about the history of their club. My aim is to prove this by asking people questions on the club they support.'

He conducted the survey, set out the respondents' answers in a chart, and wrote a conclusion:

'I asked 45 hooligans the questions and 45 quiet fans these questions. The total quiet fans' scores were 357 right answers out of 522 questions.

The hooligans' total scores were 335 right answers out of 525 questions. So this clearly shows the quiet fans have done best, getting more correct answers out of less questions, proving that quiet supporters know more about their club than hooligans.'

After a couple more short pieces of work, and after he has started a fresh project, we finally get

12 May   Today I completed my football project.

If we had been asked what manner of relating to the world projects were supposed to foster, I think we would have emphasised inquiry. Certainly, we would have acknowledged that students' needs vary, but probably we tended to count it as success when students developed out of an expressive wondering and curiosity into a more focused and disciplined examination of things. We wanted to allow full scope to the expressive, certainly in the initial stages of getting to know a topic and working up a personal sense of its meaning, but principally as the best means of encouraging a growth towards objectivity and rational procedure. Cases such as those of Brian and John seemed to afford confirmation that this was the natural way for things to develop, given the right sort of participation by the teacher. Gradually, however, I began to wonder whether most students' needs were as I had thought. The things students chose to do often seemed to suggest they were not. It is an issue I am still not sure about. The following two cases raise it in a concrete form.

Entry in Neil's log for 4.2.76, with my reply

'This may not interest you a great deal, but to me its a great subject:- FOOTBALL, but if you don't like the idea of me starting a small topic on soccer then o.k. Its a thing I've always followed and is interesting to study from its early days. But don't get the idea that I'm finished or going off studying China or going off English work. I have the books on soccer and I would mainly work on this topic at home. I won't be simply copying out of books, I just read and then write down my knowledge of the game. It probably won't interest you one bit, after all it's only a sport, what use will a subject like this be in C.S.E.? it probably won't be any use, therefore tell me before or if I start it's not much use, do you think so? Be fair, tell me your own opinion, I don't mind if you say its no use to me.

I would still do just as much or more work on China, nevertheless, than soccer. But if I do want to start a topic on it don't say yes, if you will get fed up of me talking or writing about it. It doesn't seem a serious study like worthwhile studies such as China. Is it?

Give me your reasons about why it's not worth studying, if you
think it isn't. If it's a waste of time then I won't seriously start a topic
if it's no use in C.S.E. You probably won't know hardly anything
about soccer so I would find answers for some questions myself. If I
did start a topic on soccer it may be wasting your time if you tried to
answer my questions on the game (though not many questions there
are about the game, I don't already know). I would be working
independently on the topic.'

*To answer that (i.e. would it be worthwhile and would it be OK for CSE) I'd
need to know a bit more about what you intended. You say it doesn't sound as
serious as a study of China – well, I'd say it depends how you look at it, or,
really, how broad you can make it.*

*It's to come under "Humanities", which is about people – their relationships
with each other and with the world. I reckon you*
can onto the big important issues.

Look at it this way. Soccer:
   *(1) a game – men moving a ball about a marked area according to rules. If
your project is about how they move the ball (tactics, skill etc.), in other words
about the playing of the game, that's fairly narrow and wouldn't be so good for
CSE etc.*

*(2) a game that happens in a particular society as a result of
particular features of that society etc. – e.g. the players are men
who come from various backgrounds – why is it they who have
become players and not other men? what happens to them when they are old?
how do they see themselves? what are their satisfactions? How is a club
organised, who controls it, how did they get to control it, how have clubs
changed, why, how much money is involved? etc etc – That's getting broader
and would be very acceptable. Why do some towns have teams and not others,
who started the teams, why then and not 50 years earlier – etc. etc. etc.*

*(3) a game that has a particular function in our society – i.e. what is it for?
This approach concentrates on the spectators and supporters. Why do people
get "football mad"? Why is it more than a game to so many? Why have seats
been provided since the war and not before? Why does violence centre round
soccer and not round athletics or horse-racing? Why does a society apparently
need big organised sports?*

*Quite a bit has been written on the sociology of sport, about which I don't
know much, but I could show you something on soccer hooliganism.*

*Brian has been doing a project on football which I think is a good one. Yours
needn't be anything like his but it would be worth your having a look at it if he*

doesn't mind. It interests me because it started off very unpromising and has become really worthwhile and original.

Suppose it's the game itself that you really like – particular matches, how they're played. Well, then, it seems to me you might simply want to express and communicate your response to that, by writing about it in all sorts of ways. OK – fair enough: for CSE, that would count as English, I suppose.

The Mecca project.

Tracy and Mary wanted to do a project on the Mecca dance hall. I spent a lot of time thinking about it: how could you get a purchase on an experience like that? I hoped for something 'sociological': here was an interesting social context, neatly circumscribed; looked at in the right way, it ought to reveal something of our society. I wasn't interested in them interviewing the manager or finding what time the cleaners came on; their investigation should enable them to penetrate the social significance of the Mecca, what it meant to the people who used it, what the unwritten rules were, and so on. I knocked out some questions and ploys and felt quite proud of them. I suggested ways of 'sampling' people's behaviour at the Mecca: keep your eyes on one person for ten minutes, form a general impression of the scene in a particular corner at one hour intervals, etc. And think about the ways in which the Mecca and school are different and the same — after all, there is a large overlap in their respective clienteles whose needs presumably don't change drastically between day-time and evening. My log records: 'Tracy and Mary thought my ideas on Mecca OK.'

They went away, attended the Mecca regularly, and over the next few weeks wrote their project. It showed hardly a trace of influence from my notes. Essentially it was a diary of their evenings at the Mecca, mainly about who was behaving how to whom within their own circle. It took the social context completely for granted and didn't seek in any way to see it as 'anthropologically strange'. It was full of energy and commitment, and a great disappointment to me.

I feel I was overimpressed with the need to look at reality in the light of theories or of models, to see particular cases as located in systems of alternative possibilities — in other words with the need for explanations. And I was naive in supposing that studies of particular small milieus can excitingly lay bare the underlying social bones like the fossil emerging under the palaeontologists's hammer — especially when conducted by fourteen-and fifteen-year-olds. I was fired by Berger's picture of the sociologist:

We could say that the sociologist is the man who must listen to gossip despite himself, who is tempted to look through keyholes, to read other people's mail, to open closed cabinets. Curiosity grips any sociologist in front of a closed door behind which there are human voices. (*Invitation to Sociology,* Penguin 1966)

I expected that sort of curiosity to be a potent force amongst our students. Having found sociology exciting myself, I expected them to; and some of them did. But for many it seemed that 'explanation' and 'understanding', in the social scientist's sense, we're not the most urgent needs in their relations with the social world they found themselves in.

Students who did projects on their own villages hardly ever followed the sort of 'sampling' and focusing procedures I suggested. These were clearly out of key with what the students (who were usually quite highly motivated to work at these projects) felt to be their best way in. What they wrote (and this goes also for Tracy and Mary in their Mecca project) were not inquiries which unearthed new data or revealed patterns or suggested reasons, but *celebrations.* This is my village; all this particularity, this concreteness, this irreducible hard factuality of being this way and not some other, belongs to me and I am part of it; this is the Welfare; there is where we used to play, this is what our old bread oven was like, these are some people who live here, this is what a miner does when he comes home from work, these are some often told stories about the pit, this is about my brother's whippets. The projects were descriptions, but not such as a geographer or sociologist might write; they were more in the spirit of someone recalling in loving detail what a former home was like — though in reality the writers were still living there. It was what these writings expressed rather than what they stated that was the point.

Neil, it turned out, had little wish to go into the *context* of the game of football in the ways I outlined. He never did the project. I wanted him to be sociological; I can now see that he wanted to be celebratory. Reading about the great matches and the great players, the famous strips and the yearned-for trophies was not enough: the project would be a way of extending that sort of satisfaction, a means of experiencing more intensely the glory of the game, of bringing those feelings more fully alive. Unlike the village projects, his would be celebrating a whole history. Not realising that this was what was called for, we never came up with a form in which such an ambition might be encompassed. Perhaps we could only have discovered it by letting the project get going and seeing where it led, as we did with Brian's.

Basically my mistake was to overestimate the level that students of 14-16 have reached. The way Brian and John were beginning to cope with generalisations and think in terms of systematic explanation was reflected in their emerging ability to operate the transactional function of writing; they represented a more advanced stage of development amongst our students, rather than, as I perhaps assumed, a mode of functioning which could potentially be achieved in all of them if we could only find the right triggers. It now seems surprising how hard a lesson this was for me to learn. Those two were at the point where they could optimally benefit from the sort of suggestions I was making; that mode of work was perhaps ideal for their stage. But it was not ideal for all, and the same suggestions could even have been hindering other students.

What I failed to recognise sufficiently was that those celebratory projects were themselves evidence of the achievement of some distancing and objectivity. They could not have been written at 11 or 12. Perhaps there was substance in my feeling that they were like re-creations of a former home: these students already felt themselves to be passing beyond the confines of those small worlds. I was worried at their parochialism, but perhaps the next moves would naturally have been into a wider context (though not, in practice, before the age at which most would leave school). Maybe at 16 what they were doing was what they needed to be doing; certainly investigative surveys and the like would have been of little value to them — which makes one wonder about those geography and social studies courses which build them in for everyone as the only permissible form of learning from the real world. Perhaps it is only when students have reached a certain level of abstraction in their own thinking about the world — which means the achievement of a certain distance — that they are able to be receptive to the organised general ideas that they can only acquire from outside — ultimately, from the disciplines. The best policy would probably be to promote the expressive charting and evaluation of their own worlds, while keeping before them all the time, ready to be made the most of when the moment comes, ideas and images of the world outside and of more inclusive viewpoints.

I wonder, though, whether that is right. Are scientific concepts and procedures what one 'naturally' reaches for once one has gained, by writing in the way that owes more to literature than science, a certain level of control over one's own experience? An alternative is conceivable: that that control is actually dependent on acquaintance with the scientific concepts, which need initially to be taken on trust — *un*naturally — and deliberately learnt by 'strenuous mental effort'

(Vygotsky's phrase); and that only these will provide the means whereby one can move outside one's experience and see it in more general terms. But then I ask myself, if that is so, what is the motivation to be that will make our students, who wrote those self-absorbed pieces about their own world, 'strenuously' grapple with applying sociological and geographical terms to them? I can't see it. I know that part of the method is supposed to be to introduce students to other social worlds outside their own, so that things that seemed God-given come to appear relative and they envisage alternatives: but these kids didn't want to know about other social worlds — that seemed to be one of the symptoms of their stage. So on balance I tend to think that something other than social science has to bring about the distancing which social science can then move in on and exploit.

This brings me to the final point I want to make in this chapter about the educational forms that emerged under our scheme. The difference between what I have called the celebratory projects and the inquiry projects looks very like the difference between English and the social sciences; and in fact the fate of English in this relatively integrated setting was not to die out, as so often in integrated schemes, but to flourish under the label 'humanities'. The best 'English work', to use the traditional categories, could often be found in the folders which were submitted for the Humanities CSE. The assignment of pieces of work to Humanities rather than to English was often fairly arbitrary, or had to do with considerations of assessment. The English folder tended to be used for stories and poems, writing about and around literature, and generally for one-off pieces that were not part of a longer study; thus it sometimes had the feel of a 'Miscellaneous section'.

Typically, 'English' deals with the operations we perform on our own direct experience, and with objectifying that experience at the lower levels of the scale of abstraction. It seems right that we did not draw a line according to closeness to or distance from immediate experience, assigning the more experiential to English and the more generalised to social science. It still seems to be a crucial insight that the enterprise of understanding the world — at any rate at this age — is essentially one operation, not several.

6   Cases and conclusions

Neil came into the fourth year without previously having been thought very highly of: 'pretty average grades. I wasn't doing so well in fact. Nowt special.' Nor did he see any reason to question this valuation: 'I never expected to get a top grade.' During the first few weeks nothing happened to disturb his feelings about education.

> The first five weeks in that humanities, I thought, oh well, how boring this is. I remember starting the project, me and Ivor Bell, just copying out things about the Second World War, one of the worst projects I've ever . . . I was getting nowhere with that, even though I thought I was in a way, 'cause I'd got a lot of work on it, but it was just copying directly out of books.

It was only after he had got mildly into trouble for skiving out of lessons that I seriously intervened. I suggested he try our 'unit' on China. He did, and from then on things were different.

> That's it. As if just overnight. When I got on that China project, that's what did it. Everything seemed to work for me then. I kept thinking, well, I've achieved something. I'm really interested.

When he had just started on China, I commented in my records: 'All his work so far is recording of facts, answering of worksheet questions. Nothing open-ended or reflective or imaginative.' That was dated 8.11.75. By the 15th however I am writing 'Great comments in log on the experience of reading *Red Star over China* by Edgar Snow and how he goes back to study difficult bits again. Model of right sort of motivation.' Then: '3.12.75 Terrific series of questions he asked me in the log. Really what the log is for.'

This is the log entry referred to:

28.11.1975
Today I was wondering what China might be like when Mao's reign comes to an end, whether the new communist leader will be as good as Mao (even though I dont think China could have another leader as good as Mao). Who do you think will be the new leader after Mao?

(Here he leaves a space for my answer, and after each of the questions that follow.)

I think it ought to be one of Mao's close friends who has followed Mao through all battles and things like the Long March, somebody who is very loyal to Mao, somebody who has honoured and served Mao even through hardships, somebody who could follow Mao's way of ruling China. One question I'd like to know, is whether Taiwan (Formosa) is an island run by Communists or Nationalists?

Could you tell me some other Communist countries apart from these I know (if there is any more) Poland (I think), Russia, East Germany.

I would like to know them because I want to see where Communism has spread to. A few weeks ago I heard that Communism could happen in Italy. I heard about it on the telly, I think it was on a programme called 'TONIGHT' but I forgot to watch it. I wish I would of saw it because it seemed an interesting programme. Was Russia the first Communist country?

If so what year did Communism start in Russia?

Anyway is there a chance of China being overtaken by Nationalism?

Or are the majority of people aware that China doesn't want another Nationalist government?

I understand China has now got NUCLEAR POWER and Japan has too. Japanese produced many good cars, bikes etc. But rarely do I hear of Chinese cars, bikes etc, but many plastic stuff from Hong Kong. Is China as rich as Japan nowadays?

Japan to me seems a lot more technological and up to date (than China) — is it?

The Chinese aren't a very sporting country, but one thing I know is that China have a soccer team and they soon could be official F.I.F.A. members.

I began to write in the best answers I could, found his spaces too cramped so took a fresh page, got carried away and wrote three pages.

Normally the teacher asks the questions, to be answered orally or in writing. Yet who is the one who is supposed to be wanting to know? It was good to see a student reversing the procedure and using it for his own purposes. (Later, it happened that I did ask questions for him to answer in writing, but the spirit of this transaction was very different from the usual routine.) This writing, it seemed to me, was not only instrumentally seeking information; at the same time it was expressively making a personal relationship with the topic. The writing derived from and also served to confirm Neil's commitment to the work and his sense that this was his own enterprise. Further entries from his log seem to show the same function being performed.

28.6.76

Watched a good programme last night on telly. It was the WORLD ABOUT US series which featured a documentary on the ASMAT of N. Guinea. It showed how they lived and the brilliant carvings they did. The carvings were done on trees made into poles with stories on it carved in.

These people were headhunters but law recently forbids any more heads to be taken. So the spirits are disturbed now, say the ASMAT. The ASMAT are average in numbers but are declining. White missionaries teach the ASMAT 'civilised' ways of the white living, but the ASMAT don't like this, as many fights still occur over things like cutting down a tree which belongs to somebody else. The tree isn't on his land, it's just one tree in the vast jungle. The missionaries teach the ASMAT to be Christians and are trying to get them as quickly as possible into the civilised world, so they aren't destroyed by the impatient oil seekers and foresters. The ASMAT now have jobs and are paid 50p a week and buy tobacco and stuff from this money. The carvings are in museums but the people that made them most likely will cease to exist with their old customs and traditions which are now slowly disappearing with the new life the ASMAT are being put into. They come to face pollution and other things in the new world but in their own land they never had any problems such as this. They followed the life of their ancestors and would most likely have carried on for another century or so living the life which didn't destroy them. Now it seems only a matter of *short* time that the old life of the ASMAT will disappear for good.

10.9.1976

Today an important factor in Chinese history, Mao Tse-tung the great leader of China had finally deceased at 83. All sorts of questions are now aroused on the future of this vast country. Started reading a book on Anthropology called THE TRIBE THAT HIDES FROM MAN.

23.9.1976

On Tuesday night I watched a good programme on telly. It was
called THE WATER MARGIN. Its an interesting story set in 13th
century China. Today doing some writing about the book I read
"The Cowards". After "The Cowards" is finished off I think I'll
write some notes from Fanshen, as I read through it. Then I can get
on with the primitives after this is completed, because doing them
both at the same time is a bit confusing, as I cannot concentrate
going half way through one book and then starting half of another
book without finishing the first book. I'll answer the questions on
Fanshen you gave me. The questions are a good thing, they can get
me thinking about what I've read from the book. The primitives is a
bit harder, I think, because the same things are happening to most
of the primitive tribes today and so nothing much different is learnt
between what's happening to destroy the tribes in different areas of
the world. I started this 'topic' as just a general interest in habits
and ways of living and traditions that generate in these tribes, and
suddenly I've noticed they are rapidly disappearing from the world,
like an extinct animal! I'm a bit lost for ways of thinking of the right
things to put in a topic like this.

5.10.1976

Finished my English this week on the argument between council
and public over old sheds. I was supposed to be a reporter, but my
excitement and long tale has involved me in the action and in the
end it has turned out to be a bit like a story. Not intentionally
though.

23.10.1976

Read a bit more of Fanshen. Altogether read nearly 450 pages of
this historical book. The author certainly put in some hard work in
compiling this book.

14.2.1977

Been reading a great book called "The Borstal Boy" by Brendan
Behan. It is a true account of Behan's early life. When he was 16 he
was caught in possession with detonators, wiring, timing devices etc
used for making bombs. Being an Irishman born in Dublin he
worked for the I.R.A. Anyway this book tells of how he was caught
in Liverpool and put in jail and finally taken to Borstal.

15.2.1977

Started reading a book called "The Trial" by Franz Kafka. It's a
hard book to understand because of the words in it. It is a very slow-

moving story. There isn't a great deal of interest in it. But I want to read it because he gets arrested without knowing the exact reason for arrest. He keeps asking why he is arrested but hasn't found out yet. I am on p43 and he doesn't know yet. He just attends this place like a court.

It is a very "sinister" book.

For Neil 'doing a project' consisted largely of reading; and as the reading went along he made notes from time to time (e.g. on certain chapters of *Fanshen,* though he read the whole book), and wrote regularly in the log book. He was learning much more than could be conveyed in those two forms of writing, so it seemed important that towards the end he should do some writing which would enable him to look at what he had read in a broad way, and to provide evidence for the assessors of the extent of his knowledge and thinking. We agreed between us that the best way might be for him to write answers to some very broad questions I would put to him. Thus on China I wrote down five or six questions, which he answered in the space of many pages. (One of them in fact was not a question but a suggestion that he write in the role of Mao Tse-tung looking back over his life and assessing his own achievements.) This form seemed to allow him to display his thinking to good effect; it appeared to be well fitted to the stage of development he was at as a writer. The answers, as compared with the log book entries, are moving towards the 'wellstructured essay', deploy much more information and are more sustained, but are still 'personal' in the dual sense that they present 'how I am thinking about this' rather than a detached argument which could stand on its own, and appear to express a relationship with a particular reader rather than an unknown public.

Neil's writing seems to me to convey with particular immediacy what real education looks and feels like. Watching what happened when an apparently unmotivated student found himself for the first time with active intentions relating to learning was one of my most exciting experiences in teaching. He did well in his 16+ and CSE (Grade B for English, 1 for Humanities). His success was made possible by our unconventional way of working, although he did not take advantage of all of its special features. He did not exercise his freedom of movement or participate widely in the scene as a whole, preferring to stay within a small group of friends who, according to him, talked about strictly non-educational issues:

'It was about things they'd done elsewhere, you know, in Walton like, sailing up in bathtubs up Walton canal, saying "I got sunk last night with a catapult", things like this.

Neil felt a need not to let this group down, so overtly he was one of the lads in the corner, talking, joking and affecting to have no time for school work. The educational transactions went on under the table. He worked at home, communicating with me mainly by his log and through occasional conversations which I usually had to initiate.

It was in two particular respects that the set-up served him well. There was nothing initially to indicate that Neil actually thought about the topics he was studying, still less that he might be able to an exceptional degree to use writing as an aid to his thinking. The discovery — for both of us — was made when a particular channel was made available to him for the first time, namely the log book, which was established in his eyes as a medium of dialogue by the fact that I wrote back and never marked or corrected it, only replied.

Secondly, it was a good thing that he had control over how long to keep a project running. He worked on China for the best part of the two years, breaking off for longer or shorter periods to look at other topics but always returning. He was justified by the gains he made, for although the knowledge he acquired was concentrated in a particular field (albeit one that could hardly be called narrow), the experience of going deeply into one topic and beginning to sense the underlying forces that move human societies served to carry him onto a whole new plane of awareness, so that in the long run it led to a great broadening of his interests. Neil's case vindicated our principle that wherever along the front a breakthrough is achieved, all resources should be concentrated at that point without thought for the time being of maintaining a 'balance' in the curriculum. He became interested in politics and started watching documentaries and current affairs programmes.

I started to watch the news and things like this whereas before I think I used to watch just comedy series and things like that.

He also began to read. He had been going to join the army; instead he decided to continue his education in FE. He is there now, doing business studies, economics and French (which he had dropped at the end of the third year in school). He still reads widely. In his spare time he is teaching himself Russian.

There was no question of working with Barry on the usual basis of 'You're here to work' and 'You do what you're told'. He saw himself

as a free agent, which in many respects he was; he would only work
with any commitment when he saw the point, and he exercised
considerable discretion about when to come to school. Outside, he
could and did do a man's work and generally saw school as childish.
He was intelligent and humorous, appreciated stories and discussion
and had a racy way with words. Since we had some sympathy for his
views and enjoyed his style, we did not find it difficult to avoid
approaches which would have too crudely drawn attention to his
pupil status.

We were able to keep something going with Barry for a year
without any compulsion or appeal to the work ethic. The concrete
achievements were not thick on the ground; projects were started and
then lost sight of because of absence; there were more schemes and
plans than actually initiated pieces of work. But there was plenty of
reading and discussion and there were many pages of writing. This
success, limited though it was, was made possible by the
teacherstudent relationship which our scheme provided for;
conventional ways of working would have achieved next to nothing.

The first interesting things Barry did in humanities were one-off
pieces of writing: descriptions of three different people eating their
dinners, comments on a visit we made to a road scheme in Leeds, a
science fiction story. But Barry's case is best presented through his log
book. It was in this, when it got going, that our relationship was
largely negotiated and that Barry was able to express for himself the
terms on which he saw himself doing business with education —
namely, as an autonomous consumer.

> That jot book, it were t'first thing I'd do. It were like going home, I
> mean, first thing I'd do when I got home, you know, put t'bike away, see
> how t'bike is, you know, if ever I've got nowt to do, you know, I'd go out
> and mess around cleaning bits on t'bike. At school, first thing I'd do
> were get my jot book out and started tooling it up and generally
> scribbling all over it, then now and again a flash of inspiration would
> come. Sometimes I'd have nowt to write about, I'd just put summat in
> just for t'sake of it . . . That jot book, though, it were real, that.

I should describe the log's appearance. It consists of two ordinary
school exercise books, one brown and one green. Only a few pages of
the second one, the green one, have been used. The first one is full,
apart from the last 14 pages which contain elaborately lettered
slogans or graffiti: THE WHO, BAZ, BAZ + M, BARRY + , BAZ + MAZ,
FOCUS BY FOCUS, QUEEN, "THE" "WHITE NOISE" and various
drawings and scribbles. Volume 1 (brown) is dropping to bits; it is

pierced with eight holes, made by a hole-puncher, and at one point a cross shape has been cut out of the cover, which is completely covered with scribbles, writing and drawing. Inside, the typical page has a margin, drawn freehand in biro, or none, writing which moves about the page according to no clear principle, multiple underlinings, stars and asterisks, arrows, and varieties of patterns and doodles up the sides and between the entries.

The log entries transcribed here are from two sequences, the first up to February 1976 and the second starting May 1976. Entries by me are in italics.

At the time of the first entry Barry was doing a project on bridges. Earlier I had written that I would show him some bits of Leonardo's notebooks — I had a vague idea that he might do something on the same lines.

Wednesday 12 November
Tidied out my file and wrote up this log for you to read. And started story.

Much appreciated. I've written some comments in your folder.

Memo: Leonardo.

Your writing's great – I can't get enough of it. It's very clear and definite and you always have a definite point of view. Do you enjoy *writing?*

I know where you could go to get quite a few bridges in one go:

(I drew a sketch map)

When are you off?

Never if I am put in a fridge. NEXT WEEK probably, but how do I get there, walk, run, bike, car, taxi, bus, train, plane, ship, rocket, or shot out of a cannon?

On yer bike!

Monday 17th November
Can't remember what I did for sure but I did read some of that book (Child of the Jago) or summat.

Wednesday 19th November
Wout and drew some bridges in Walton.

Friday 21 November
Went on a trip to Sheffield — smart time.
(a few entries omitted)

Friday 5th December
Finished off story about one of my first encounters with the middle
class and read some sheets about sociology.

Monday 8th December
Finished off the drawing of the railway bridge I started and started
a story on bridges.

*Right. Now do you think you might find some sort of sociology project more to
your liking?*

I'll think about it. Yes, maybe if I could go taping and write about
it, tape about 2 or 3 people from each estate and write about what
they were like and what I think of them.

Wednesday 10th December
Started reading book that Mr Medway gave me called The Gates
by Mildiner and House. And read some stuff about the working
classes with Mr Medway. That book The Gates, it's good.

*This log is getting good too. I think we might be onto something good with the
project we were discussing. Should be pretty proletarian, eh?*

What does that mean?

Friday 12.12.75
Away

Monday 15.12.75
Read some more of the book called The Gates from 20 to 34 and
stop using those big words. (arrow to 'proletarian')

Some big words can tell you things you can't learn any other way.
I thought you'd remember Lockwood's 3 types of workers – proletarian,
deferential and privatised. 'Proletarian' means to do with the traditional
working class – industrial workers in heavy industries.

Take The Gates home for Christmas, huh? (Something to do on Christmas
Day. You don't want to be writing all the time.)

(arrow to 'Christmas Day') Who are you trying to kid?
(in margin) very funny

Wednesday 17th December.
The Boss keeps on and on about "Leonardo". I thought he was a
painter, but anyway *he* keeps on about some writing *he* gave me of
his. *He* didn't, or I can't remember. Read some more of the book
"The Gates" (34, 37) and started story on Walton people. The Boss

is trying to con me into doing my notebook like "Leonardo da vinci's", he'll be lucky, "sociology", maybe, but Leonardo etc. etc. no way. I do things my way — but I may have a go on Friday or after the Christmas holidays. Also been reading some Open University story with *him* — about cab drivers and tipping. And wrote all this lot.

Evening, Barry. Yes, I reckon you're on the slippery slope towards education – better watch it or they'll have you, boy.

I think a sociological notebook's a great idea – thanks for suggesting it. You don't have to do it like Leonardo da Vinci – after all, he was only some 15th Century nut who painted the Mona Lisa and invented a helicopter and analysed muscle-structures etc. – we can do better than that.

Item for sociology notebook:
You meet a woman walking round a school. How do you know she's the school secretary and not a teacher?

I jot down 2 pages of other suggestions

(Added later) I bet you never read all that, did you, you monkey? 27.1.76

(A few entries omitted)

Wednesday 14 January 1976
Done some more of the doctor's surgery and read some of the new book "It's like this cat" and thought about what else I am going to do for a topic in the future.

Sociology. People of Walton. Etc.

Would you be interested to see some sheets on deviants (drug-takers, soccer hooligans, criminals etc. etc.)

Yep

Do we need another long talk to get you going on something?

Doubt it.

Friday, 16 January, 1976
Why couldn't I go to see Mrs Hope today, because I have to be home for 3 o'clock.

Because she was giving a talk at the time.

Yes I would like a sociology project on Walton people. But when can I go down there and talk to about 2 people in a morning taking notes and then coming back and writing up what I think they are like and so on. I have done the end of that story "The doctor's surgery" and read some of the Beaverbird book with rest of them.

Your doctor's surgery thing was OK. Walton – whenever you like (in hums. time) but you must work out what you're going for exactly. It'll take a bit of thinking about.

About a week I think to give me a rest from all the *work* I have been doing.

I like your log.

I carved it myself.

(A few entries omitted)

28.1.1976 Wednesday
I would like to do a small project on the countryside (pollution of it etc. etc.) but I think I'll need your help with the questions.

Yes.

I think the idea of walking out with the tape, camera and wellies *all* day and writing it up later on the next day and taping some of my comments and taking pictures and kicking mixi-rabbits and so on. Can't think of "owt" else to write "abart" so I'll stop now and wait till tomorrow.

We need a bit of advance planning here. You're otherwise engaged Friday, so the next time would be Wednesday (half day).

You said you'd write about going out with dog and the gun, which could be a winner.

"ow" much?
I'll sell it to you.'

Barry wrote the piece:

A walk in the country.

There are two main ways for me to go out with the "dog and gun" into the fields and woods. One is along the canal to the second bridge over it and along the road to the Fern Wood. On down the field to the beck and up the hillies and down the path past the forty acre field to the swamp or up the hillies and through the wood. The

wood has been ruined by [farmer's name] the fat pig who owns it.
He lets sheep and horses roam about it eating the bark and killing
all the trees, it's all littered with dead, rotten, dieing, trees. He
sprayed two conker trees in the 40 acre field, with a killing stuff, but,
the massive conker trees had fought it off and within 6 months they
had new buds. The Bone Patch used to be an adventure with
rhododendron bushes and brambles all over, but now it's just
another walk. I won't tell you about the dog and gun, just about
what's happened to Walton's countryside. At the end of the wood at
the top end is a metal fence, and all along the edge of the wood is the
wood wall and the fence starts at the wall. About 2 or 3 yards after
the fence is the "Gates". These have been rotted and kicked away
and are built into the wall. Then down the other side of the wall and
over another stile and by now you must have noticed the massive,
dirty-great stinking black mass, called, the outcrop [opencast mine],
in all its great sweaty glory. What a dump. The only part that's left
now is the swamp and half of that's gone. It won't be anything like
good land now for another 10 years after they have finished there.
Then you climb over the fence and over the *Red Beck*, and on to the
new footpath around the edge of the outcrop and over the stile at
the end of it, down another path and into the good old *Fern Wood*.
This has been ruined by all the horses churning the footpaths to
mud and shit, the wood is good though. It is quiet but now you can
hear the outcrop a lot, so everything looks as though it has been
ruined. Then through the Fern Wood and along the canal and
home, a good meal, a cig and you feel really good sat in front of a
blazing coal fire.

Log again:

4.2.76
Was late so couldn't go round the Fern Wood with cassette, camera,
wellies and flat cap — but I've been told that Critch [Graham, the
teacher] has been reading *my* log book and he said it was *very Good*.
What do you think of that then?

He's easily* impressed. (Barry's asterisk) *He had a lot of trouble reading it,
actually. Ever thought of improving your handwriting?*

I can't help it if the junior school didn't teach me to write properly,
and if I tried to write neater I would go so slow you would only have
about a story a year.

* not that easy though, just one story, and he knew an *expert must*
have written it.

Handwriting. It would be slower for a time, but probably only 2 or 3 weeks, then you should get back to normal speed again.

Thursday, 12 February, 1976

Went down Allerton Bywater pit, *very good,* I *must* write *another* piece of work, this time on the pit we went to. That piece of work of yours [I wrote a piece about the pit visit] was *quite good for a beginner* — HA HA — and I enjoyed it, and about my writing, I think it's only as bad as yours and I can *read* my writing better than I can read yours.

In May I showed Barry, along with a number of other students, the poem *The Nail* by Vasko Popa. I asked him what he made of it. He got more out of it than any of the others and agreed to write about how he saw it.

The Nail

One be the nail another the pincers
The others are workmen

The pincers take the nail by the head
With their teeth with their hands they grip him
And tug him tug
To get him out of the ceiling
Usually they only pull his head off
It's difficult to get a nail out of the ceiling

Then the workmen say
The pincers are no good
They smash their jaws they break their arms
And throw them out of the window

After that someone else be the pincers
Someone else the nail
The others are workmen

(Yugoslavian poem translated from the Serbo-Croatian by Anne Pennington)

from Geoffrey Summerfield (ed) *Junior Voices: the fourth book,* Penguin Education

'What makes me think this poem is about people and Communism is that the Nail has a head and the pincers have arms and jaws. The "Nail" is a rogue element, a person who is against the system of government. The "pincers" are the people in office, the leaders and so on. The "Workers" are just the ordinary people who decide who gets the leader's job by voting and so on. The pincers have to get the Nail out, and stop him from changing people's minds, to his advantage. And when the government realise they cannot get him out by ordinary means they "pull his head off". In other words they put more pressure on him, and frame him and so on. So he got shot or jailed, but the people don't like that so the leaders are chucked out, and somebody else takes over, only to have the same thing happen again and again. It's like children, they'll fight like hell to be the part in a game they want to be, then when they get fed-up with playing that part, they'll fight like hell to play a different part.'

Log again:

26th May
Be thinking about what you want to do after the hols.

What do you suggest? sociology, countryside?

No, I've a better idea. I'll tell you.

If it's deciphering those bloody daft poems of yours, then you can go and fly away.

I think you'll like Chris James this aft. You'll probably find his centre pretty interesting too. (The idea referred to was to interview the warden of a field studies centre, not because of his job but because he was someone I thought Barry would find interesting to talk to.) *Aim to get a good piece of writing out of it.*

Blackmailer

Remember to make the log a record of what you do as well as an Old Codgers Column.

Cheeky pig I'm no old codger whether you are or not.

E.g. would you care to comment on the book I read on Wed. ("Manchild in the Promised Land" – Claude Brown); also on how you feel about finding you can suss out tricky foreign poems.

I really dig sussing out frog and nazi and any foreign poems like that one, The Nail. I liked that "Manchild" thing it's good, it starts quick and keeps on going. Yes I did enjoy being brainier than any other person in the class, when I cracked that coded Czech poem. Oh yes and I don't fancy the idea of yours of working the balls off me till I get a grade one "A". So there.

Where the hell were you on Wednesday?

2.7.76
Listen, colonel. On Chris James, your writing was OK but when you were talking to me you got really good, didn't you? You said things to me this afternoon that I bet you'd never said before in your life and probably hadn't even thought. You were great. It's a winner of a project and I'm quite excited about it.

After he had said so much more in our conversation than he had put down in his writing about his interview with Chris James, Barry rewrote and expanded the piece. Here are the opening and extracts from the rest:

An interview with Chris James, Warden of the Wakefield Urban Studies Centre

It was a bright and hot sunny day, and as I walked down the entrance, I noticed that the building was one of those 19th century stone boxes, and had been cleaned, as nearly all the public stone buildings had around Wakefield. It looked very good. I walked in and the smell of schools nearly knocked me flat, you know, that kind of peppery sort of smell. I walked in and saw all these kids running around, and a few were from Walton I noticed. I found out later then that school kids come on visits to the place often. Then, towards the far corner of the big room I was in, I saw a man, casual, ginger beard, fair hair, fairly placid looking, and talking to a group of young kids. Ah, Chris James, I thought. Even though Mr Medway had given me a rough sort of idea what he looked like, I couldn't get this sort of picture out of my head, that he was bald on top, fat lazy and grumpy, grey haired as well, but he was just the opposite of what I thought. As soon as he saw me he said, "Ah you must be Barry." This stopped me dead, nearly any way. I realised Mr Medway must have got in touch with him and described me to him a bit, but to just come out with it like that without the slightest hesitation, "Well," I thought, "hell, we got a right one here." . . . just by saying that like he did made me feel he was honest and open, and I knew I was going to get on well with him, I said back to him, "yes I am, you must be Chris James, Mr Medway asked me to come and do an interview with you, for a sociology project at school", "ah yes that's right" he said. Then we started walking around the place talking and after a few minutes we went out with the kids, to the graveyard across the road, while they did some "brass" rubbings on the grave stones and so on, we sat and talked about him, mainly and his views and attitudes to life.

Barry reports at length on what Ray said, then comments:

He lives on a new estate in Walton and has those type of neighbours that think themselves posh, but are skint everyday of the week through paying for the car and the house. He is the only person on the estate who hangs out washing, all the rest have these "hot air dryers" that dry them in the house, so nobody else can see what they've got. He also has vegetables in the front and back gardens, whereas all the neighbours have lawns and roses, all trying to keep in the social status of life. . .

I think he is just being his self, nothing to put on, nothing to put off. I think he isn't as bloody daft as the others as well, not by a long way as daft, because he isn't conned by the producer into buying a clothes dryer that costs, say, £200 to be in line with the rest of them and which breaks down after 2 years so you have to buy another. He just used the wind which is free, but against the system of most people, but most of the people isn't him. They think he's common, and he's one of a seemingly dying race of people who believe you live your life the way you want to live it, not the way of the system or anything like that, but you have a certain number of years to live your life and it's there, now, and you can do what you want to do with it.

Soon after that it was the summer holidays and then Barry did not reappear.

> Eventually I just thought, bugger it, I'm not staying in this chuffing hole, that's it now . . . I thought, what the bloody hell am I doing here? get myself up to t'farm, like, you know, I'm not going back to school for a bit.

It was Christmas before they got him back off the farm and into school. He wrote little and did little for the rest of his time. On the last day, however, he wrote in his log:

So here it is squire, the last day, 5 years of waiting and it seems all but a flash, as everything else does. Been good the last two years (well less ½ year at the farm and so on) the sense of humour, those NHS specs, rent-a-nit beard, ah well, that's life, come back some day eh, go round to your house and have that bike ride eh? I've enjoyed writing in here, have you? See you some day, eh, see you.

The importance of Barry's case for me lies not in the gains that were actually achieved, which represented only a beginning, but the possibility it reveals of a different way for education to come to school-rejecting working-class adolescents — a way that by-passes the usual over-serious, oversupervised, authority-tainted procedures. Barry, Neil and a few others created a black economy of the classroom, dealing in education for fun and satisfaction. All it required to come into being was for us to allow ourselves to be used as a service by the students, selectively and on their own terms; to make the good things of education available without imposing them. It was with these students, with whom the alternatives were to deal the way they chose or not at all, that we came closest to realising our ideal of an education voluntarily taken up for the sake of the manifest benefits it offers.

I can't help feeling that basically Barry had got it right. He had no illusions about the charade of schooling in general. Because of his strength of character and his supporting home culture, and no doubt because he had managed to miss so much school, his intelligence and curiosity had survived intact and he remained untouched by all efforts to make him feel a moral obligation towards school work; so when he worked, the work was simply the direct means towards satisfaction of his impulse to understand or create or simply amuse himself; in it there was no suggestion of the ritual performed to gain praise, grades or a feeling of righteousness.

Unlike those who rejected the whole show as 'all just school', Barry had a nose for the bits that had real value. He showed that it was possible to pick out the parts that have significance for oneself without buying the whole package offered by school, according to which enlightenment *can* be won, but only through the proper channels and after the long weary march through the syllabuses. Those gifts which bestow an access of power and competence on the student — the illuminating knowledge, the grasp-extending skills — are generally sold in school only at the price of submitting to modifications in one's behaviour and attitudes; modifications which are in the interests of social control and of a workforce fitted for a rational-bureaucratic economy, but not necessarily in the interests of the individual. Undergoing them may kill important potentialities in oneself. To have instilled habits of tidiness, orderliness and systematic diligence, not to mention docility, in Barry (by what means I cannot imagine) might have been a service to 'the economy' but would have meant no gain for Barry: no increased power to understand and control his situation would have flowed from it. He showed up the falsity of school's insistence that education derives from 'good student' characteristics and established that it is, on the contrary, entirely compatible with not having a 'sensible attitude', or a proper folder, with not coming to school every day, not looking after books, keeping your anorak on in class, chewing and putting your feet on the table.

Clearly, I am aware that organisation and assiduity are essential to certain kinds of worthwhile enterprise; but there is a difference between developing them for oneself in order to be more effective in pursuing a purpose of one's own, and having them instilled as *moral* qualities and obligations in themselves. I am not saying that Barry developed those qualities that way either, but at least he kept alive and strengthened some others: energy, directness in going for what he found worthwhile, adventurousness in thought, and skill in seeing the wood for the trees and going for the essential insights without getting bogged down in irrelevant 'study'.

In taking up certain educational offerings, Barry sacrificed nothing that was important to him. He successfully fitted education into the varied adventure of his adolescent life. He continued to sparkle in the social life of the classroom; as Neil said of him, 'Barry could get on with anybody really. One time he'd just be writing away there, then he'd merge in with us. He could change, you know, straight, one thing to another.' And he was free to go out every evening.

A colleague who taught humanities according to the same general principles to the year group below the one I am describing concluded afterwards that 'Shayhill was, in essence, the embryo of a state of learning which, fully developed, could have created something near a practical and vital platform for working-class kids to grow and liberate themselves.' Unfortunately it did not occur to us systematically to find out what the students themselves thought until the very end of the course, when we asked those we could find to answer a questionnaire for us.

Responses were generally favourable. People approved of the friendly and uncompetitive atmosphere, the easy relationships and the individual attention. Many said they had learnt a lot (though much of it would be no use in a job); the point already made about equipping people to talk effectively was made ("It also prepares you for work as you find you can talk freely to anybody and not feel nervous"). The main reservations were about pressure to work — many felt there should be more pressure — and control of those who did not want to work, though there were few suggestions as to how. Some said the unmotivated should be segregated, but the weight of opinion was emphatically against streaming or setting, even though it meant that each group might include members who did not want to work.

Some of Nick's answers were:

I think that the teaching method was wrong. I think instead of humanities we should have had separate lessons of Geog, History, RE, and English.

I think that you were right in having mixed ability groups. It makes the lessons more better working with different ability mixed (?) people.

I think the humanities teachers are soft and do not show enough discipline in the class.

I think Humanities teachers enjoy teaching students but I don't know why.

There is a lot of time wasted in Humanities, mainly caused by teachers not making pupils work. If you waste time and you want a good job well you had it, but if you don't want a good job it does not matter wasting time.

I think the atmosphere in Humanities is boring and depressing.

I think the Humanities for the last 2 yrs has been run terrible.

Humanities has made me aware of the society around me.

The views of the majority were closer to Sharon's:

For me the method has done me justice. It has taught me that I have to work to get what I aim for.

Because the groups were not split into ability groups it gave the people of a lower standard a chance to get to know the people of a higher standard. This was good as the people of a lower standard can always learn a thing or two from the people who are perhaps more intellectual than themselves. It didn't have any drawbacks because as has been mentioned the people worked at their own level, though I did hear one or two people say that they were being pulled down with being put in with "the dunces".

The attitude between student and teacher in humanities is a good one. It is friendly, and enables any child to speak to a teacher as a friend. The teacher in this subject does not insist that you work, he just does his best to encourage you. Because of this humanities is different to other subjects. I think it is a good kind of relationship especially as most of the teachers share a few of your interests. If the teachers share your interests you don't find yourself saying;
"Good morning sir, nice weather today."
Instead you approach and say
"Hiya Graham, did ya see Status Quo on T.V. last night?"

This kind of teaching gives a better and more enjoyable relationship altogether.

Humanities lessons shouldn't be solely for work. Discussion and conversation are two important things which have to take place. If teachers and pupils aren't allowed to talk throughout lessons the school is so silent and unfriendly.

The atmosphere is friendly, sometimes noisy but enjoyable. I think this atmosphere is good and I do approve. Sometimes though because of the atmosphere I do have difficulty in settling down to work but because I have taught myself discipline I have to go into another classroom to work or let the atmosphere go straight over my head and settle down and do the work to do. Everyone talks to everybody else and very rarely you see people arguing. More often than not everyone is cheerful and smiling.

Humanities has been a good lesson and one I have always looked forward to. It has been run in such a way that the pupils have found a responsibility for themselves.

It is worth adding that the examination results in Humanities (and in History and Geography) were satisfactory, and in English were highly satisfactory, with about four times as many gaining the O Level grade C/CSE grade 1 standard as in previous years.

In insisting on giving great weight to students' intentions and purposes, so that if they were to enter into a new way of working or form of relationship it would be by choice and with their eyes open, we accepted that we would not always be successful, and so there were students, as we have seen, who apparently never took a look outside their own social world, and others who would have benefited from getting in with other groups but who could not be brought to leave the three or four friends they habitually sat with. To make options available but not to impose, and thus to risk this sort of failure (but what guarantee was there that other methods would succeed?) seemed the only way that was consistent with our educational aim of autonomy, with our procedural conviction that only chosen activity would produce sufficient motivation to power the intellectual effort, and finally with our ethical attitudes to our students: treating them as responsible agents was the only basis on which we could avoid doing violence to ourselves, let alone to them. (We felt this increasingly during the second year when we had to deal with students who had irrevocably decided that none of this was for them.) The achievements of some students were entirely due to our relatively non-coercive relationship; and in the majority we had a body of selfrespecting students who looked as if they were alive, ran themselves and behaved like free individuals. Whatever else we had or had not managed to do, we had lifted the curse of student passivity. The attitudes and responses of the students, and the new types of work and new possibilities of student release that were beginning to emerge, confirmed our conviction that choice was the factor that made all the difference.

It was choice, in fact, that counted rather than another element we had thought to be indispensable, namely an intense sense of purpose: we had made too much of that in our original vision. Starting from a picture of switched-off students routinely turning up at lessons and doing their 'average and below average' work without any of it affecting them, we had believed that only powerful purposes of their own would suffice to reawaken the dormant powers. We learnt, not that purposes are not essential, but that they can be gentler and less dramatic than we envisaged and yet still capable of lifting students onto a new level of operations. The animating intention need not be a searing need to know: it could be, for instance, an amiable desire to send up some piece of pretentiousness, or a playful wish to construct an imaginary world. Students with whom our approach was working and who had found things they did not need to be pushed to do did not give the impression of being possessed by a mission; they simply had an air of knowing what they were there for. They took part like the rest in the good life of conversation and dropping in on friends in other groups, but they acted as if they had something else to go back to; and when they returned to the work, in class or at home in the evening, they picked it up with pleasure.

With a few students there was perhaps the one topic above all others that was the key to releasing their powers of inquiry. But while particular topics often got students started, we sometimes felt that others would have served equally well. It might have been more feasible than we had originally supposed to satisfy the needs of many of the students out of a restricted range of topics which we could have resourced fully and carefully — always provided that there was scope for the students to find their own ways through them, and that in the last resort they were free to reject them and pursue something quite different. Topics in the face of which students had switched off on conventional courses turned out to be successful with us when they were presented as material for exploration, evaluation and dialogue. What it needed was a different sort of process whereby they were able to take a more satisfying and autonomous role in relation to the material.

The crucial distinction was not between the intense thirst for knowledge and a gentler 'interest' — both would serve — but between activity undertaken by choice and activity performed as mere routine. There were indeed cases in which nothing short of a breakthrough was called for; but more often a range of involved activity in a lively climate, with periodic moments of intensity, seemed a more appropriate model to work for.

Ours was a curriculum devised to meet one overriding need: to get students actively involved in their own education. In working to get this right, we barely started to develop other important practices. In particular there was too little of the cooperative work — writing groups, publishing teams etc. — which we admired in some English departments. On the other hand we were aware that students in those schools usually enjoyed that type of opportunity for only five periods in an otherwise traditional, 'transmission'-dominated week, whereas we had 'liberated' a huge tract of the curriculum. Understandably, we were not able to exploit the full possibilities of this situation from the word go; it would take time to work on our own skills and our students' expectations. But in the long run we stood to be able to create something which, because it extended across a wide area and 12 periods on the timetable, could make more of a difference to the students than anything which could be achieved within the narrow frame of the English allocation. And a group of students whose participation in cooperative work would be worth having because freely given seemed a good basis to start from.

It was towards more cooperative work that we certainly needed to move. In the event, we did not develop in this or in any other direction because we did not continue to operate the scheme after the end of the two years. This was largely because our institutional base was eroded because of changes in examinations, groupings and timetable. There was also informal pressure, explainable partly by the climate of insecurity induced by the 'Great Debate' and the reactionary pronouncements of HMI's and others, for streaming and separate subject teaching. It seems, looking back on it, that what we did was made possible by an adventitious combination of circumstances: a school not yet under full academic pressure and an enlightened CSE board. We found ourselves in a small clear space which we had no right to expect, and we exploited it to do things which went against the trend of the times. It will be harder in the next few years to do anything of the kind.

I still feel committed to most of the notions we acted on. The abandonment of class-teaching in the usual sense, except as an occasional resource, is long overdue; and the alternatives seem inescapably to imply longer time-blocks, which can of course only be achieved by some sort of pooling of subject time. The diffusion of 'English' into other areas can produce great benefits without necessarily endangering the distinctive core. Freedom to talk and to write in varieties of ways are undoubted necessities, as is a large measure of student discretion in general. The doubtful area is how forcefully you can push students into particular topics and activities. There is little room for dogmatism here since constraint is built into the whole school situation from the start. I'm prepared to be convinced that I could justifiably have been more pushy than I was, though I'm inclined to believe that I would have done more harm than good that way. In any case, the issue only arises in this polarised form if you start with fourteen-year-olds; if you have been working up to it from the time the students were eleven, which we were not able to, it is likely that such things as focused cooperative activity would be second nature.

What happened was not especially remarkable. In another climate — if, for instance, the late sixties had continued instead of turning into the mid-seventies — experiments like ours would probably have proliferated and ours would have been in no way outstanding or worth writing a book about. But in fact it was and remains highly exceptional, and this is the reason for my making such a meal of it. Surely there is enough suggestive evidence from the few such curricula that have existed to justify at least some further experiment. Things are undoubtedly harder now, but isn't there room in the education system — the pride of which is said to be diversity — for a few more schools to try finding gaps in the examination system, blocking their time, freeing English from its earmarked compartment and operating on a basis of student consent?

Chameleon is a freelance publishing group which specializes in educational books. The six members of the group all previously worked at Penguin Education, and banded together in 1974 to form Chameleon. They have published a short series called **Standpoints** with Oxford University Press; and their **English Project** series was published by Ward Lock Educational Ltd.

This new series, Chameleon Books, is being published in association with Writers and Readers. Each book deals with a key and sometimes controversial educational topic of the moment, and is written in a clear, personal but readable manner by an author with involvement in the subject, and practical experience to draw on.

WORKING WITH
WORDS
Literacy beyond school

Jane Mace

Why are 2 million adults in Britain illiterate? Do they lack ability
and application, or has our educational system let them down
somewhere? Why is the adult literacy movement starved of funds
and existing mostly on voluntary labour, while educationally
privileged institutions like universities eat up money?

In Jane Mace's powerfully argued and provocative book she looks
critically at our attitudes to literacy, the complex learning relationships between tutors and students, and contrasting methods of
literacy work. She backs up her argument by drawing in detail on
the experience, the writing and the opinions of literacy students,
whose voices are so rarely heard in such discussions. Her book
challenges teachers, at school as well as in the adult literacy sphere,
to question many of their traditional assumptions about literacy.

Jane Mace has worked for eight years on the Cambridge House
Literacy Scheme in London, one of the pioneering organizations in
the recent adult literacy campaign. This is her first book.

case   ISBN 0 906495 14 8
paper ISBN 0 906495 15 6

CLOSELY OBSERVED
CHILDREN
The diary of a primary classroom

Michael Armstrong

This is a unique book: a meticulous description of a year Michael
Armstrong spent in Leicestershire in an 'informal' primary school,
documenting the intellectual growth and development of children.
Going way beyond the conventional researcher's role, he made
extensive daily notes, and worked with the class teacher to analyse
in detail the children's learning. The results of his remarkable
investigation put flesh on the bones of what we know about
children's classroom behaviour — the book draws heavily on the
children's own work as well as the records of teachers and of the
school. It is sure to prove a major contribution to our understanding
of children's understanding.

Michael Armstrong taught for several years at the internationally
known Countesthorpe College in Leicestershire. This is his first
book.

case   ISBN 0 906495 04 0
paper ISBN 0 906495 21 0

BEYOND
CONTROL?
The causes and effects of
school suspension

Rob Grunsell

We know all too little about how and why children get suspended
from school. Is it mainly a get-out for headteachers under pressure?
Is there a class or ethnic bias amongst those who are punished in this
way? Why do some schools use suspension more than others? Rob
Grunsell, armed with detailed information from one London
education authority, unravels the many threads of this complicated
and emotive question. In particular, by means of extended
interviews with many who have been suspended, he puts the
children's side of the question, and asks whether it is not often the
schools themselves that have failed to create the right learning
opportunities for these children. His book will pose many serious
questions for parents, social workers, and other agencies who have
to work with children removed from school in this way.

Rob Grunsell worked until recently in a unit for suspended pupils.
He was one of the founders of the Intermediate Treatment Centre in
Islington, which he described in his widely acclaimed book,
Born to be Invisible.

case   ISBN 0 906495 22 9
paper ISBN 0 906495 23 7